KEEP THE FAITH

A STORY OF TRIUMPH, TRIAL, AND TRUSTING GOD FOR THE IMPOSSIBLE

Keep the Faith
Copyright © 2018 by John and Terina Dutton.

All rights reserved. No part of this publication may be reproduced, distributed, or transmitted in any form or by any means, including photocopying, recording, or other electronic or mechanical methods, without the prior written permission of the copyright holder, except in the case of brief quotations embodied in critical reviews and certain other noncommercial uses permitted by copyright law. For permission requests, write to the publisher, addressed "Attention: Permissions Coordinator," at the address below.

ISBN: 978-1-64318-006-9

Front cover image by Kim Carano.
Book cover design by Jeff Summers.
Interior layout design by Kristen Polson.

Imperium Publishing
1097 N. 400th Rd
Baldwin City, KS, 66006

www.imperiumpublishing.com

KEEP THE FAITH

A STORY OF TRIUMPH, TRIAL, AND TRUSTING GOD FOR THE IMPOSSIBLE

John & Terina Dutton

"Write the vision;
make it plain on the tablets,
so that a herald may run with it.
The vision awaits its appointed time;
and it will be fulfilled.
If it seems slow in coming,
wait patiently;
for surely it will take place;
it will not be delayed."

—Habakkuk 2:2-3

TABLE OF CONTENTS

Forward: Gideon's Fleece 9
Chapter 1: The 1st Prophecy 13
Chapter 2: Nevada 19
Chapter 3: John Dutton-QB04 27
Chapter 4: NFL Draft, A Dream Delayed 33
Chapter 5: Hello John, This Is Jimmy Johnson 37
Chapter 6: Bring Your Playbook 41
Chapter 7: The Happiest Place On Earth 47
Chapter 8: New Beginnings, And A Dead End Road ... 51
Chapter 9: God Said So 59
Chapter 10: There Is A Rebound Coming 67
Chapter 11: The Bowl Is John's 73
Chapter 12: Audience Of One 83
Chapter 13: And You're Going To Win 93
Chapter 14: Fields Of The Fatherless 101
Chapter 15: The Word Tested Us 113
Chapter 16: Entangled 119
Chapter 17: Forget It Forever 125
Chapter 18: Beulah Beach 135
Chapter 19: A Single Speck Of Dust 143

Chapter 20: He Chose The Foolish 151
Chapter 21: A Kernel Of Wheat 161
Chapter 22: Yet Lower Still 169
Chapter 23: What Is It.......................... 175
Chapter 24: Do Not Give Up 185
Chapter 25: Believe 169
Chapter 26: Success To Significance 193
Chapter 27: What Are You Busy With 199
Chapter 28: Step Into The Promise Land 207
Chapter 29: Miracles Will Happen 215
Chapter 30: Write The Vision 229
CONCLUSION: Don't Give Up 235

FOREWORD

GIDEON'S FLEECE

"I will place a wool fleece on the threshing floor" Judges 6:37

"Here are my instructions for you, based on the prophetic words spoken about you earlier. May they help you fight well in the Lord's battles. Cling to your faith in Jesus Christ, and keep your conscience clear.
For some people have deliberately rejected this, and as a result, their faith has been shipwrecked." 1 Timothy 1:18-19

(TERINA): In the spring of 2011, I sat in the stands at John's game, questioning how we would rebound from John's injury. It felt as though we couldn't go any lower, but there was no way up as well. We were floored. John recently tore his Achilles at the ripe age of 36. We were further from the Promise than ever. How could God possibly expect us to believe he meant John would put up the numbers again in the NFL!

We must have this all wrong, I thought to myself. God couldn't possibly mean the NFL. While we had received confirmations along the way,

I reasoned they either had to be a coincidence or God changed His mind since our faith fell short. Maybe we were a modern day version of Israel, wilderness dwellers, who would end up dying before receiving the promise because of doubt and unbelief! (Hebrews 3:19)

Had our lack of faith failed us? Had God given up on us, his wandering sheep, long ago? As I sat in the arena, wrestling with everything, I decided I needed a sign so clear I could not question the meaning of the prophecy anymore. I needed to know once and for all *exactly* what God meant. I needed a fleece.

In Judges 6, we read about Gideon, who asks God to give him a sign that God was really going to do what He said. Gideon says, "If you will save Israel by my hand, as you have said, behold, I am laying a fleece of wool on the threshing floor. If there is dew on the fleece alone, and it is dry on all the ground, then I shall know that you will save Israel by my hand as you have said." Sure enough, the next morning when Gideon checked the fleece, the ground was dry and the fleece was wet. Then, to be sure it wasn't a coincidence, Gideon humbly requests another sign. This time, laying the fleece on the ground, he asks God for the fleece to remain dry and for the ground to be wet. In Judges 6:40, the Bible says, "God did so that night and it was dry on the fleece only, and on all the ground there was dew." The Lord graciously gave Gideon the confirmation he needed. On that night, I needed a "Gideon's fleece" of my own.

The stands happened to be the first place I had ever heard God speak, so I prayed, "God, please, if we have it all wrong, just tell me to get over it, to move on, drop it, let it go, or that we're idiots. I can take it. I just *need* to know either way. We lay this Promise on the altar, like Abraham with Isaac, and I raise the knife to end this Promise once and for all, just tell us either way: Is it time to move on with our lives, or is John going to play in the NFL...not the IFL, AFL, CFL, or any other FL. Are we supposed to keep the faith in believing you mean the NFL specifically, or do we forget it and move on with our lives?"

For the rest of the game, all I did was pray, wait, and listen for God's reply...but I heard nothing. After the game, a stranger walked up to us on the field and randomly said, "You know, miracles happen." Though it was an endearing gesture, it was nothing more. I was looking for clouds in the sky to form into words saying "Yes" or "No" or something close! After the traditional post-game routine of autographs and pictures with fans, we left the stadium to go home. As we drove away, my heart broke into pieces as I faced the reality it was over. God had never answered me.

As I fought back the tears, I told John about my wrestle with God at the game and how it was over. All of it. The Promise, as well as the other prophesies and confirmations we had received over the years, were merely a coincidence, nothing more. It felt like we had driven down a road for 12 grueling years, only to find out it was a dead end. What a waste of time!

How would I ever know how to discern God's voice again? How would I ever know He was speaking? My faith felt thoroughly shipwrecked. I didn't doubt God was real; I just doubted my ability to hear Him.

I felt so badly for John and all I had put him through. For years, I encouraged and challenged him to keep the faith and to stay the course. Every time he was down, I would remind him of the word and the various confirmations we had received along the way. I wouldn't let up until I saw His faith in the Promise rise again. I'd quote verses on the phone to him after a rough game, saying, "Do not grow weary in doing good, for, in due time, you will reap the reward, *if* you do not give up."

I'd insist, over and over, "John, God is faithful. He has a plan for you in football. He said so. Keep going, keep believing, keep the faith."

Many times our faith made us look like idiots, like Noah building a boat in the middle of a desert. I felt so much despair. As I looked away, expecting a deafening silence to follow, John, with an incredulous tone to his voice, said, "I didn't tell you what happened."

Instantly, my heart started racing as I turned my head towards him, asking what happened. John told me, "I was standing by myself when a fan walked up to me and said, 'I have a message for you.' I asked from whom, assuming it was from the team doctor or the media, but he calmly looked up and pointed towards heaven to say, 'From God.'"

"Are you serious?!" I interjected. "Oh my word, what else did He say?"

He didn't say anything more, but handed me a wooden plaque with a cross etched into it and the words, "Keep the Faith."

I was completely dumbfounded.

(JOHN): At this time, I had no idea Terina had prayed for God to send a fleece, a confirmation for us to stand on. I accepted the plaque, put it in my bag, and finished signing autographs. I had no idea the significance of it until Terina explained exactly what occurred between her and God in the stands.

(TERINA): I reached into his bag and pulled out the plaque. As I looked down at the words, I couldn't believe my eyes. I ran my fingers across the letters carved into the wood, Keep the Faith, and contemplated all God had to orchestrate to inspire a fan to deliberately hand-carve a plaque, with a message from God, saying, "Keep the Faith," then bring it to the game, and give it to John, at the same time I sat in the stands, pleading with Him for an answer.

In over 13 years of playing well over 200 games, nothing like this had ever happened. We didn't get the words, forget it, get over it, or move on, which I was somewhat expecting; the writing in the clouds, the fleece we got was, "Keep the Faith!!!"

CHAPTER 1

THE FIRST PROPHECY

"For prophecy never had its origin in the human will, but prophets, though human, spoke from God as they were carried along by the Holy Spirit." 2 Peter 1:20-21

"The one who prophecies speaks to people for their up-building, encouragement and consolation." 1 Corinthians 14:3

(TERINA): The story surrounding the Keep the Faith plaque began 12 years before, one beautiful fall morning at a small church in Reno, Nevada. We had no idea, as we headed to church that morning, the very course of our lives was about to be changed forever. It was 1999, and John had just been just released from the Cleveland Browns during training camp. He had broken his foot and needed surgery, so we returned to Reno where he could start post-surgery rehab on his foot and I could finish my senior year as a swimmer at UNR. Soon after arriving, we started attending a church we'd heard about from other athletes on campus.

As we walked in, we found a seat as normal, but I noticed there was a guest sitting in the front pew. Once the service started, the head pastor introduced him. He explained how our guest, who was a pastor, had the gift of prophecy. Prior to his message, he planned to call a few people up on the stage, as the Lord directed him, to speak a prophetic word over him or her.

When he took the stage, he explained what prophecy was from a scriptural standpoint, as well as what prophecy was not. He explained how divination and fortune-telling were an abomination to God, but how prophecy was a gift of the Holy Spirit (1 Corinthians 12) used to edify and encourage the body of Christ. (1 Corinthians 14). He emphasized that everything he said should be tested by the word of God, and that a genuine word from the Lord never contradicted scripture. While it seemed biblically sound, I was completely unfamiliar with prophecy. Even though John and I had both grown up in Christian homes, and had attended church most of our lives, this was completely new to both of us. We sat there feeling guarded, yet intrigued. On one hand, we didn't want to be like the Pharisees, who ultimately rejected what God was doing and who He sent, simply because it didn't fit into their personal understanding or interpretation of the scriptures. However, we didn't want to be led astray either. Was prophecy still relevant today? I thought to myself, "If prophecy is intended to build up and encourage believers, why wouldn't it be?"

While I remained cautious, I prayed the Lord would give us wisdom and not let us be deceived in any way. I also figured there was no way, out of the entire congregation, I was going to be called up anyways, so I resolved to simply observe from the crowd.

All of a sudden, I saw the pastor pointing our way. I immediately turned around to stare at the people behind me, thinking maybe he meant them and we would somehow get out of this. However, they stayed in their seats and stared at us. I slowly turned my head back around, straining my eyes to see if he was still looking our way: He was not only looking our way but also zooming in on us. He had our number! John and I studied each other's faces. After a long pause, we slowly made our way to the stage, my heart beating out of my chest the whole way.

(JOHN): The only thing I remember is I had no idea about prophecy. Though I definitely had doubts initially, I was open. Since I had never heard of a personal prophetic word before, I didn't know what to expect.

(TERINA): Similar to Saul's Damascus Road experience, where he was going along his way when the Lord's voice stops him dead in his tracks, changing the course of his life forever, we, too, were about to have our Damascus road experience. We had simply been going along our way with no idea God was about to suddenly invade our little world, and make known, as He did with Saul, the plan He had for our lives.

As we got up on the stage, the visiting pastor prayed over us. Then he began to prophesy.

"There was a man named Jacob that I wrestled up until the point that his hip was dislocated," he said. "No I didn't injure you, but I supernaturally allowed this injury to slow you down. I am going to touch you, and I am going to lay a foundation for a surprising success that is going to amaze you."

My entire insides were turning. What did that mean? He continued, "This has been the most insecure 18 month period you have ever known... but you will put up the numbers again."

Eighteen-month period, I thought, what was 18 months ago? I would have to figure it out later as I needed to hear every single word he said. He wasn't going to stop so I could deliberate what he was saying.

"You're going to look back and say this was the best thing that ever happened to me." This injury? Ummm? That's an interesting thought.

"The only thing worse than success is success without me, and I spared you from that, says the Lord!"

"What is this guy talking about?" I thought to myself. Success without Him? I love God. How would we ever have success without Him?

After many other words, he concluded. "I will never ever pull my promises away from you, never ever says the Lord. Watch and see what I do in this hour as you follow Me. Watch and be amazed."

A few others prayed and prophesied over us on that pivotal day, but even now, I can hardly remember anything they said. When the service finally ended, we left hurriedly. I was so eager to pick John's brain to see what he thought about all that had taken place and to write down every word so we could begin to make sense of the prophecy. While I could not articulate exactly how I felt, I knew that what just happened was *significant*, though at the time I had no idea why.

(JOHN): Unlike Terina, I initially had no idea this was going to be so significant in our lives. I should have taken it more seriously at the time, but I just didn't fully grasp the concept of prophecy as being a word from the Lord. Terina asked me if I remembered what the pastor had said: I honestly couldn't recall anything.

(TERINA): Being given the prophecy was like being handed a large puzzle with no photo on the front and a thousand pieces inside that would somehow fit together to make one large picture. It would take years to even begin to understand what each piece represented independently and where it fit into the bigger picture.

Though we have yet to see the final piece or even have a set timeframe for when it will happen, we knew it would eventually make perfect sense when the full prophecy was fulfilled. Until then, this journey would challenge us to "Keep the Faith"—every single day as we waited to see what God was going to do. Though we would find ourselves still waiting nearly

20 years later, the path to the NFL began much before the prophecy or the plaque ever existed. It was during John's senior year at the University of Nevada, where he first discovered his dream of playing in the NFL was soon going to become a reality.

CHAPTER 2

NEVADA

"For I know the plans I have for you," declares the LORD, "plans to prosper you and not to harm you, plans to give you hope and a future." Jer. 29:11

(JOHN): As I headed into my senior year at Nevada, I could hardly believe I was one season away from my lifelong dream of making it to the NFL. I was more determined than ever to finish my college career by having the best season of my life. Even though 1996 was a very successful season, I felt I had a lot to prove. We had made it to the Las Vegas Bowl the previous season, but I hurt my thumb on my throwing hand and was unable to finish the game. I hadn't trained this hard to sit on the sidelines during the biggest game of my life up to that point.

As I headed into my final season, I had plenty of unfinished business. There was definitely a buzz around the community, on campus, and in our locker room. Everyone had us picked to win the conference for the second straight year. Both my team and I personally received some votes in the national polls. The previous season, the Nevada offense was ranked

#1 in the country in Total Offense, #2 in Passing Offense, and #2 in Scoring. I was ranked #5 in Passing Efficiency ahead of quarterbacks such as Peyton Manning, Donovan McNabb, and Jake Plummer, and was #2 in the country in Pass Completion Percentage. In order to best prepare for my senior year, I decided to stay at Nevada over the summer to train. I had no idea, God had other plans for me that summer as well; I was about to meet my future wife, the one who would help carry my faith through the years to come.

(TERINA): The first time I noticed John on campus was at the end of my sophomore year. We had a class together that required accumulating volunteer hours over the course of the semester. One of my best friends, Rick, who was like a big brother to me, wanted to find out who this guy was I told him I spotted in the class we all had together. Neither of them attended class often because, of course, they were so committed to their volunteer hours, so Rick never discovered he knew this guy. One day, while reading the *Sagebrush*, the school newspaper, I discovered this mystery man was the quarterback. My initial thought was, "*Oh, great! The football players are already cocky, and, being the quarterback, he's probably the worst!*" I knew Rick would tell me whether or not to steer clear. When I told him it was John, Rick, surprised me by saying, "Man, he is a great guy!"

I began to see him at a Bible study for Christian athletes, which really drew me to him, as it was very important to me to find a guy who shared my faith in God. Having recently recommitted my life to Jesus, my mom and I prayed over the phone, asking God to give me the patience to wait for the man God had for me and to not to settle for anything other than that.

(JOHN): With both of us being athletes, I started to see Terina around campus a lot, whether it was in class, the weight room, or at the

Bible study. One day I was sitting at the shuttle stop on campus when Terina walked by. I told my teammate, who was sitting with me, "There's something about that girl." Of course, I was attracted to Terina, but there was something else about her I couldn't quite explain. Looking back now, God was at work.

(TERINA): One day during summer, I was working out in the weight room when John and Rick came in to work out together. I personally think John was stalking me since he suddenly began showing up in the places I was, but in all seriousness, they both came to train for the upcoming season. I do question Rick's commitment to training as he spent every minute of his workout teasing me, making inappropriate gestures towards John while spotting him, and intently looking in my direction.

(JOHN): After my workout with Rick, who was a teammate of mine, we talked about Terina. He told me that I should at least ask her out on a date, so he gave me her number. I went home both excited and scared to death. I was never one to go out on a lot of dates. Up to that point, I had a girlfriend in high school and only a few dates after that. This was not my thing. That night, I sat by my phone and stared at it until I mustered up enough courage to dial Terina's number. After I heard "Hello," I asked if Terina was there. The girl who answered said she would go find her. Great, more time to think about this. Before I could hang up the phone out of complete fear, another girl came on the line.

"Hello," she said. "Hi, this is John." "John who?" Oh my gosh, what was I doing? Why does dating have to be so hard? I introduced myself and asked her out on a date for the following night. When she said yes, a sense of relief came over me. As soon as I hung up the phone, I started planning the date.

(TERINA): The funny thing is, I knew exactly who was calling me. Rick told me John asked for my number. I knew there was a chance he would call, though I didn't want to get my hopes up. When the phone rang, I answered it, but I wasn't ready to talk to him. I was so excited, so I pretended to go and "find her" while I ran and told my roommates it was him. Once they helped me calm down, I came back and "answered" the phone. He asked me on a date for the following night, and I said yes.

(JOHN): From the very first date, it was as though I had known her for a long time. I felt completely comfortable around her. We both knew quickly we were going to get married. We hadn't thought too far into the future yet as to what we would do once I graduated. I was gearing up for my senior year of football, and Terina was getting ready for the swim season. In between workouts, the weight room, and the training room, we spent every available minute together. Looking back now, God's timing was perfect. He knew I would need her in the season ahead and for the others that would follow.

(JOHN): I had set some high goals for our team and also for myself before the 1997 season, but that all changed with one hit. We had a 1-1 record going into our 3rd regular season game against the Oregon Ducks. We were in a back and forth battle when, late in the 3rd quarter, an Oregon defender hit my shoulder as I let go of the ball.

At the time it hurt like crazy, but I didn't think much of it and finished the game, losing a heart-breaker in overtime 24-20.

As I reached the locker room after the game, I tried to take off my shoulder pads but noticed I couldn't even lift my throwing arm. After I had someone help me take off my pads, I slowly undressed and showered. After my media interviews, the trainers checked me out and put a bag of ice on my shoulder. When I woke up the next morning with a lot of pain and no improvement, I went to the training room to get re-evaluated. I did the typical ice and stim treatment and spent the following week in the training room.

Although I felt better as the week went on, I knew I was nowhere near 100%, and my dad suggested I get an MRI. The results came back that I had a severe AC joint separation. My focus was just getting back on the field for the next game, but my dad was extremely worried for the long-term effects of the injury and tried to convince me to keep that in mind.

We travelled to Mississippi to face the Southern Miss Golden Eagles. Since I would do anything I could to help my team win, I decided to take a shot prior to the game to relieve some of the pain in my shoulder. I warmed up and felt pretty good, but unfortunately, the effects of the shot wore off about 2 series into the game. When I dropped back to throw a curl route, the ball went about 10 yards straight into the ground. I knew immediately I could not continue to play, as I would only be hurting the team. We ended up losing the game 35-19. We had just slipped to 1-3. I had no idea if I would be able to play the next week or even the rest of the season, for that matter. The excitement of the 1997 season had just been snuffed out.

Because my shoulder did not improve at all during the next week, my coaches made the decision to start the back-up quarterback, Eric Bennett. We headed out East to play the University of Toledo. The coaches had me dress out even though there was no chance of playing, so I thought. In the second quarter, Eric hurt his ankle but pushed through and played through the injury until early in the 3rd quarter when he severely twisted his ankle again and had to leave the game.

With the lack of depth at the quarterback position we had that year, I was next in line even though I could not throw more than 5 yards down the field. At this time, there was no press about my injury or why I didn't start the game. So I trotted out on the field like nothing was wrong. We had a very good run game to go along with our passing game, so we ran the ball for a couple of series and then ran a few bubble screens where I basically shot putted the ball out to the receiver. Then a pass play came from the sidelines. I told myself to take my drop and go through my normal read, but when I threw the ball, it went straight into the ground about 5 yards in front of the line of scrimmage. My mind was telling me to throw to the tight end 12 yards down the field, but physically, I just could not do it.

Right then, Coach Tisdel, the head coach, told the offensive coordinator that we would not be throwing any more the rest of the game. He did not want to risk any more damage to my arm. We entered the 4th quarter trailing the Rockets, yet we had to run the ball, every play, for the rest of the game. Late in the 4th quarter, the defense was laughing and mocking us since they realized I couldn't throw the ball. We lost the game and dropped to 1-4 on the season.

When we came back on Monday, I found out that Eric's injury would cause him to miss the rest of the season. With Eric out and me barely at 50%, things did not look good. We had a bye week, and with a week off and a lot of rehab, I felt a lot better.

We lost our next game, going to a 1-5 record, but in spite of the frustration we all felt, we actually still had a shot to meet our #1 goal—to win the Big West Championship and go to a bowl game. Conference play was starting. If we won the next 5 games, we would still qualify for our 3rd consecutive bowl game.

During the next 4 games, our offense came to life. We averaged 52 points and won every game decisively. The Wolf Pack was back to playing our kind of football. Going into the final regular season game, we were 5-5, one win away from the conference championship. We ended up losing 38-19 to end our season. What started out back in the spring as a season with a lot of promise and hope ended with a lot of disappointment.

As I walked out of Mackey Stadium for the last time as a player, I knew I would never play another game on that field. Though I was named

Big West offensive player of the year for the second straight season, was third in the country in Total Passer Rating, and sixth in the country in passing yards, I felt I didn't live up to the standard set from the other quarterbacks who had gone before me. In the end, a player and a team are measured by wins and losses. Finishing the season 5-6 was not the ending to my college career for which I had hoped. I was disappointed about that. Overall, I cherish my time at the University of Nevada. I built many lasting friendships, and, more importantly, I met my wife. My faith and trust in God was not as strong during those years, but looking back, I can see how God was already moving in my life, slowing me down as the future prophecy would mention, to write a much bigger story than I could have ever imagined. For now, however, I was attempting to forge ahead with my own dream. My next stop was the NFL—at least that was my plan.

CHAPTER 3

JOHN DUTTON-QB04

"We can make our plans, but the LORD determines our steps."
Proverbs 16:9 NLT

(JOHN): After the final regular college season game, I took a couple of weeks off to rest my body, particularly my throwing shoulder, since I was never able to give it a chance to heal during the season. I also began the process of looking for an agent so I could start preparing for the pre-draft workouts as well as the Senior Bowl game.

(TERINA) During his meetings with quite a few different agents, one agent in particular stood out. This agent pitched himself as the agent who could transform a QB from being a middle round pick to a 1st round draft pick. The other agents concentrated more on their post-draft role of the player's career, how they would negotiate the contracts, as well as endorsement and investment opportunities they would provide. This agent had a more intentional approach towards properly preparing his clients for the NFL Scouting Combine and pre-draft workouts. John would have the opportunity to workout with some of the top trainers and coaches in the country. By doing so, he hoped to increase his performance at the Senior Bowl and NFL Combine. As a result, interested NFL teams would invite him to personal workouts, which would result in elevating his draft stock.

(JOHN) SENIOR BOWL: My first post-season stop was at the Senior Bowl in Mobile, Alabama. At the time, the Senior Bowl was the premier all-star game, coached by NFL coaches. Nearly all NFL coaches, general managers, and scouts attended at least some portion of the week. The teams were comprised of the best senior players from around the country. It was an honor to be on the roster.

I came knowing I had a lot to prove. I played at a mid-level college, and even though I ended my college season with good stats, our team did not have the best record. Unfortunately, scouts take that into consideration, especially at the quarterback position.

Before the Senior Bowl, I had moved up to Santa Monica to train, which was arranged through my agent. Every day I would workout in the weight room and train with a quarterback coach. I did everything I could to put myself in the best possible situation.

At the Senior Bowl, the week of practice is more important than the game. This is where the coaches and scouts truly have the opportunity to evaluate your talent. However, due to the rains that week, the practices were cut short. Since we ended up practicing indoors on makeshift fields, it was somewhat difficult for each player to showcase his ability at the NFL level. The game itself was a lot of fun. While I felt I played well, I still left knowing I had a lot more to prove.

After the Senior Bowl, I headed back to Santa Monica to continue preparing for the NFL Scouting Combine only a few weeks away, which would be intense. It is a weeklong showcase where college football players, who must receive a personal invitation, perform mental and physical tests in front of NFL coaches, scouts, and general managers. We were tested physically on our size, strength, speed, mechanics and pretty much any and everything else that would correlate to our potential on a field. We were mentally and emotionally tested through interviews, personality testing, and more. Our performance results during the combine would directly affect our draft status, salary, and, potentially, our careers.

On the day of the NFL Combine, I arrived as John Dutton but quickly became QB04. From the minute I arrived, I was pulled in a million different directions. Media interviews, NFL team interrogations, and physical demands from all the testing made the week exhausting.

The physical is the most extensive medical exam you can ever imagine. It included 6 stations with approximately 5 team doctors at each station. NFL teams check any preexisting injuries that you've had, probably since high school. They also want to know if you are susceptible to injuries. Like with any other investment, you have to do your due diligence. They didn't want to invest in a player who had a high risk of injury. At every station, each potential NFL player has a complete physical exam—not just one exam, but six. And as a quarterback with an injury to my throwing shoulder, the doctors spent an extensive amount of time tugging my shoulder in directions I didn't even know it could turn. I knew my shoulder still wasn't 100%, but after all the exams, my shoulder felt like it was going to fall off.

I tried not to think about how it would affect my performance the following day when I would have to throw in front of every NFL coach, general manager, and scout. I had to prove that my shoulder not only was a non-issue but also would allow me to perform at the NFL level.

Throughout the weekend, teams would find me, QB04, and bring me in for an interview. Some would talk football and get me on the board to draw up X's and O's, testing our knowledge of the game; some just wanted to talk, to get to know me as a person. It was very intimidating sitting across from some of the coaches I grew up watching walk the sidelines on my TV, but it was a great experience to see them and to talk to them in a different setting.

Going into the field workouts, I felt confident. Since I knew I had prepared for this moment, I went out and did my best. I ended up running the 2nd fastest time in the 40-yard dash for a QB (4.62), and I did well in the shuttles and the broad and vertical jumps. During the throwing drills, I felt I had a lot of zip on the ball and made some good throws. All said and done, between the interviews and the on field drills, I thought that I had put myself in a very good spot heading into the personal workouts.

After the combine, only a couple of months remained until the draft. These couple of months would be critical in either improving or hurting my draft status. Once the combine is finished, every NFL team starts to solidify their draft boards and puts a final grade on players. They have evaluated players on film, at the all-star games, and at the combine. If there were certain players in whom teams were specifically interested, they had more opportunities to get an up close and personal view of each player.

Prospective draft picks also participate in either their college team's Pro Day, or their own personal workout where they invite teams to come to their college to watch their workout.

Twelve different NFL teams came to watch my personal workout. From the feedback my agent received from them, I had proved to be a higher round pick. The team that showed the most interest was the Jacksonville Jaguars. They could not make my personal workout, but the offensive coordinator, Chris Palmer, personally flew out to Reno to meet with me. We sat and talked a long time, and we just played catch. I felt that Jacksonville would be a great fit; I also got the feeling that Coach Palmer thought the same thing.

A few weeks before the draft, the Miami Dolphins and the Jacksonville Jaguars flew me in for personal visits. While I didn't work out while I was there, I toured the facilities, met the coaches, other current players, and sat with the quarterbacks coach to talk about life and football. This is also a very critical evaluation because the teams are trying to get a feel for who you are personally, and if you would be a good "fit" for the team.

My first trip was to Miami where I met with the assistant coaches and had a short visit with head coach Jimmy Johnson. Growing up, I had always rooted for the Dolphins because Dan Marino was my favorite quarterback. It was an honor to be able to spend some time there and meet the coaches and some of the players. Because Dan was winding up his career, I thought going to the Dolphins could be a good fit. Even though they brought me in for a personal visit, I never got the impression that Miami was very high on me. They hadn't come to my personal workout, and my agent had never really talked to them.

My next visit was with the Jacksonville Jaguars. In Jacksonville, from the very first moment I arrived, I had a completely different feeling than in Miami. I felt that they were very interested in me. I connected well with the front office personnel as well as the assistant coaches. I also had a long meeting with the head coach, Tom Coughlin. I loved the facilities, the team, and the city. I could really see myself playing there for my entire career.

I certainly had Jacksonville circled as a team that would draft me. In a few weeks, I would know for sure. Little did I know I had only begun my journey of unknowns. Soon enough I would discover God had a much different plan from the one I had constructed for myself. The process of learning this painful lesson was only beginning.

CHAPTER 4

NFL DRAFT, A DREAM DELAYED

"This has been the most insecure 18 month period you have ever known...but you will put up the numbers again." ~1st Prophecy

(JOHN): Waking up the morning of the NFL Draft was surreal. I had dreamed of this moment my whole life—the day when I would officially become a player in the National Football League. Ever since I was a young boy, I wondered if I truly had the talent to go to the NFL and now I was expected not only to be drafted but also possibly as early as the 1st round.

Since signing with my first NFL agent a few months earlier, this had become my primary goal. I could hardly wait for the draft to begin. With a draft party planned at my parent's house, family and friends began pouring in for the soon-to-be celebration.

(TERINA): The air was thick with anticipation and excitement as everyone talked, ate, and waited anxiously for the draft to officially start.

Keep the Faith

When the time arrived, everyone quickly settled into their seats to watch, wondering what team would select John as their future quarterback.

Every time a team was up that John felt was a possibility, everyone, especially John, held their breath. Though it was a pretty lofty goal, it wasn't entirely impossible for him to go as early as the 1st round in the draft. His hopes were high. As the first round came to a close, his name hadn't been called. While he was secretly a bit disappointed, no other quarterbacks after Peyton Manning and Ryan Leaf had been chosen either, so he wasn't too concerned that another quarterback had been taken in his place.

As the day progressed, pick after pick went by. Before we knew it, well into the 3rd round, John still hadn't been selected. The sound of talking and laughter that had previously filled the air was replaced with a tangible uneasiness as everyone sat glued to the television silently wondering, "What is going on?"

(JOHN): Obviously, I wanted to be picked in the 1st round. As the 1st round ended, I wasn't too upset because I was certain my name would be called in the next 2 rounds. As the 2nd round came and went, only one other QB had been drafted, so my anticipation continued to grow as we headed into the 3rd round. I just knew this was the round that would change my life. I couldn't wait to hear my name being called, as I finally became an NFL quarterback.

Half way through the 3rd round, my agent called and said he had been in contact with a few teams and felt very optimistic it was going to happen this round. We were about 3 picks away from the 86th pick, the Jacksonville Jaguars. This was the team with whom I felt the most comfortable. I really had a good feeling I would soon be heading to Florida as a Jaguar.

As the 86th pick came up, I had the same feeling in my stomach then as I had before every game of my career. I sat by the phone waiting for the call that was sure to come any second. Before the phone rang, however, I saw the announcer walk to the podium and announce, "With the 86th pick of the NFL draft, the Jacksonville Jaguars select Jonathan Quinn, Quarterback, Middle Tennessee State."

What? My stomach went from butterflies to feeling like I had been kicked in the gut. What just happened? I couldn't believe it. It felt like hours before my agent called me. He told me that even though the assistant coaches wanted to draft me, Tom Coughlin, who favored Jonathon, ultimately had the final decision. As I sat there in utter disbelief, my agent informed me that the Broncos, who were in a position to draft a QB, were coming up in 5 picks. This could just as likely be the spot. I tried to put the devastation of the Jaguars pick behind me and focus on the Broncos' pick. As the 91st pick came in, the phone never rang, and that was not good news. I couldn't even watch this time as I heard, "With the 91st pick of the NFL draft, the Denver Broncos select Brian Griese, Quarterback, University of Michigan." I literally felt like my legs went weak and my heart sank. The 3rd round ended with the next pick and the 1st day of the draft was over.

Shortly after the draft ended, my agent called and assured me that teams in the 4th round were sure to select a QB. While he said my name was at the top of the list of the remaining QBs, it didn't make me feel any better. My family and I were just sitting there in awkward silence as I wondered what to do next. Do I thank everyone for coming? Do I slip out the back door?

Awkward.

It felt like another nail had been hammered into the coffin of what seemed to be a dying dream. When I did not get selected on day 1 of the draft, I began to feel the real possibility my name would not be selected at all.

CHAPTER 5

HELLO JOHN, THIS IS JIMMY JOHNSON

*"Therefore the Lord waits to be gracious to you,
and therefore he exalts himself to show mercy to you" Isaiah 30:18*

(TERINA): At the end of the first draft day, John surveyed the room where his family and friends were gathered for his "celebration." Though he knew his family was supportive regardless of how the draft went, he *felt* like a failure, not only letting himself down but also everyone else.

(JOHN): So many questions entered my mind at this point: Am I not good enough to be in the NFL? Had I already played the last game of my career without knowing it?

Honestly, so much of the personal disappointment I felt was due to the expectation of what could possibly happen. In some experts' opinions, I was projected as the #3 QB in the draft behind Peyton Manning and Ryan Leaf. Because of this, hopes were high for everyone, mine in particular. My agent had also invested a lot of money in my training as well, so I felt the pressure of not letting him down. I didn't want to waste the time and money he had invested in me.

Expectation can be such a dangerous thing; the higher the expectation placed, the further the fall when things don't go as planned. All I knew was my entire life of football, the training, games, weights, film, overcoming every obstacle, injuries, and challenges, came down to this moment in my life. When it didn't go as I had hoped, it felt like my lifelong dream partially died. It is one thing to dream of doing something impossible; it's another thing entirely when you are one moment away and it gets snatched right out from under you. It was hard to swallow.

I knew how fortunate I was to be among the small group of men who would ever get the opportunity to go further than college football, but it is never easy when something you have sacrificed so much of your life for doesn't unfold the way you imagined. While I was grateful to be one of the few players to be drafted from Reno, I also carried a failed dream inside, making the day disappointing as well, though I never openly expressed it.

(TERINA): My heart hurt for him, I knew how it felt to watch something you have worked so hard for suddenly disappear. Having trained my entire childhood as a gymnast, I understood the life-long pursuit of a dream and all of the sweat, blood, and tears that went along with it. Most of my childhood was spent commuting almost 2 hours a day, 5 days a week to and from practice, where I spent 20-25 hours weekly, year-round, from 9 years old on. The pursuit was costly, but I dreamt of the day it would all be worth it.

The summer before my freshman year of high school, I had finally reached the pinnacle of the sport: I was an Olympic-level gymnast.

One day at practice, I was doing a dismount on beam when my foot slipped off the side and rolled, causing me to fall to the ground. In upper level gymnastics, if you wipeout on any skill, you immediately get up and do it again before fear can set in. I jumped back up onto the balance beam to do it again in spite of the pain, but when I took the first step, I realized it was really injured. Much to my coach's dismay, I jumped down onto one foot and hopped over to the corner, where I sat down and cried. I knew it wasn't just a minor injury. In fact, this injury would ultimately end my gymnastics career. As soon as the reality settled in that I was no longer chasing my Olympic dream, something died in me, though I didn't recognize yet. It was the death of my Olympic dream. Now, watching John sit there, I recognized what he felt, and I hurt for him. We decided to go on a run to burn off some steam. So we strapped on our running shoes and took off. We stretched in silence and ran in silence, just thinking about everything that had happened that day.

It took a little bit for the disappointment to wear off, but he finally eased into bed that night knowing tomorrow was a new day, the second day of the NFL draft. He still had a chance to be selected by a team.

The next day, a smaller group of family and friends arrived; still hopeful John would be selected. As the second day of the draft began, people gathered around the television to see how it would all unfold.

(JOHN): As the 4th round came and went, I could no longer even watch the draft. Though no other quarterback had been selected, doubts and questions continued flooding my mind. Did I not do enough? Am I not good enough to play in the NFL? After the 5th round concluded, I faced the reality of not being drafted at all.

We were about midway through the 6th round, when my phone rang. I was certain it was my agent. I answered the phone and heard, "Hello

John, this is Jimmy Johnson. How would you like to become a Miami Dolphin?" I couldn't even believe what I was hearing—the call I had been waiting for finally came! I told him I'd love to become a Dolphin and thanked him for selecting me. He passed me off to another coach who filled me in with the details. They would be getting back to me soon about the upcoming minicamp the next week.

As I hung up the phone, we all rushed to the TV to see my name get announced, "With the 172nd pick, the Miami Dolphins select John Dutton, Quarterback, University of Nevada."

The excitement immediately came back. We all celebrated and cried. The Miami Dolphins! The team I had rooted for since I was a little kid. My sister, Janelle, ran into a closet at my parents' house to retrieve an old Dolphin Starter jacket I received when I was a kid. We went out on my parents' deck and took a picture together. Right in the middle was the old Starter jacket.

The biggest emotion I had was relief. The waiting was over: I had a team, and my NFL journey had officially started. My mom brought out an old address book I had as a child where I had written in Dan Marino's name and fake information as though I really had it.

The dream of every young boy watching his favorite athlete is to get to meet him; now I was going to be on the same team, practicing side by side with one of the best quarterbacks to ever play the game. It seemed unbelievable.

Though it didn't turn out as I had originally planned, I knew it was an incredible gift for which I was genuinely thankful. I also knew I still had a long way to go before I would make it through camp and into the season, but I wasn't thinking too much about that. For now, it was time to celebrate.

However, I had no idea just how long that road would be or how many detours and dead end streets I would come to along the way.

CHAPTER 6

BRING YOUR PLAYBOOK

Extraordinary afflictions are not always the punishment of extraordinary sins, but sometimes the trial of extraordinary graces. God hath many sharp-cutting instruments, and rough files for the polishing of His jewels; and those He especially loves, and means to make the most resplendent, He hath oftenest His tools upon. ~Archbishop Leighton

(JOHN): The day I headed to Florida, I still couldn't believe I was a player on the Miami Dolphins. It seemed surreal. After all the years of playing football, from Pop Warner through college, my dream of playing in the NFL had finally transpired.

Once I arrived at the Dolphin training facility, I was measured for a helmet and handed a bag full of workout gear, shoes, and a jersey. Walking into the locker room, I found the one with my name. I stared at it in a bit of disbelief. Was this real?

We had an 8:00am meeting, so I hurried into the quarterback meeting room and took a seat.

As I looked through the playbook I just received, the door to the meeting room opened. I turned around to look as one of the quarterbacks walked in. As I stood up to meet him, he stuck out his hand first and said, "Hello, I am Dan Marino." Really? Oh, that's who you are. I've only had your name and "phone number" in my parents' address book since I was 10 years old! I don't

remember what I said at that moment. I just hope I didn't make a fool out of myself. As the meeting started, I had difficulty staying focused; I was in the same room as Dan Marino, one of my all-time favorite quarterbacks.

At the start of training camp, I knew there was no guarantee as five quarterbacks were fighting for 2 or 3 spots, with Dan Marino clearly securing one. The first few days were up and down. If you are not a top draft pick, the coaches do not have a lot of patience with you. I was excited after the first scrimmage. I thought I played very well, going 6 for 6 with one touchdown. I thought it would be enough for the coaches to take notice, but the next day I barely got any reps in practice. It frustrated me: one quarterback barely played, and the other threw two interceptions. I, however, was the one that got my reps cut. I wasn't sure what else I could do but continue to go my hardest each day and try to get better.

A few weeks later, as I walked into the locker room, a staff member approached me to tell me, "Coach wants to see you. Bring your playbook." I knew that didn't mean Coach Johnson wanted to go over plays with me; it meant my time with the Dolphins was over. I was getting cut. As

I walked upstairs to Coach's office, I had a sick feeling in my stomach. Sitting across from him, he told me that they were going to keep three quarterbacks, ones with experience. I shook his hand, thanked him for the opportunity, and left the office. When I returned to the locker room to get my personal articles, the reality of the NFL hit me square in the face: My locker had already been cleaned out. They didn't waste any time making room for the next person. It was a reality that was hard to swallow.

After leaving the building, I made phone calls to Terina and my parents. My agent called me shortly after to inform me about the waiver wire and to be ready to go to another team. After a player is cut, he goes out on waivers. For a 24-hour period, teams have a chance to select the player. After the 24 hours is up, the player becomes a free agent. While I was heartbroken, I knew that I had an opportunity to get picked up by another team.

The Atlanta Falcons picked me up off waivers, and I headed there for training camp. Terina decided to stay behind to continue training until we knew whether or not I would make the team. She found an excellent swimming coach in Ft. Lauderdale who had trained some of the top sprinters in the world. It was a great place for her to wait.

About a week into training camp, Terina came to visit me. As a couple, we had decided we would never go more than 2 weeks without seeing each other. I also wanted to show her around to give her a feel for the place we would possibly call home. I really liked it there.

While the nature of being a professional athlete means you never know how long you will live anywhere, we were still young and naïve. We drove up to Lake Buford and imagined the possibility of living there. We thought about how fun it would be to have our families come to visit us in this beautiful place if we stuck around long enough.

(TERINA): The cuts were the very next day. John wasn't allowed to leave his hotel room until all the cuts were made. Since I had nowhere else to go, we sat there quietly and waited, curtains closed, as though we were in hiding. We tried to listen intently to what was going on outside the door between the coaches and the other players.

(JOHN): During the wait, it felt like the clock was not even moving. All around you heard the knocks on the door as dreams were dashed. While I waited, different scenarios ran through my head: Was I going to be the 3rd quarterback, would they put me on practice squad, or would I get cut? As the hours went on, I thought maybe I was safe. But, just then, the knock came.

(TERINA): Since I wasn't supposed to be in the room, I jumped up and ran to hide in the bathroom behind the shower curtain. I stood there in complete silence, hardly breathing, attempting to hear every muffled word through the closed door.

(JOHN): I dreaded answering the door, so I hesitated, took a deep breath, and then opened it. The coach came in and talked to me briefly. He said, "Coach Reeves wants to see you. Bring your playbook." My heart sank. I got the same sickening feeling as I did just a couple of weeks before in Miami.

As I sat in front of Coach Reeves, he explained that they would love to bring me back in a week and put me on the practice squad. It meant I would get cut right now, but when the regular season started, I would likely get signed again. I came back to the room and told Terina she could come out of hiding. I explained the situation, and then we packed up my things and made a plan to move back to the West Coast.

For the next week, I waited for a call from Atlanta. I continued to train and get ready to be on the practice squad, but as the final cuts came in and the regular season was about to start, I never got a call. When my agent called the Falcons, they said that they had some injuries in their final preseason game and their plans for the practice squad had changed, which meant they were no longer going to bring me back. I couldn't believe it. What seemed like a great opportunity just turned into another disappointment.

From the high expectations of the draft, to not hearing my name until late on the 2nd day, to suiting up as an NFL player for the first time, to getting cut by the Dolphins, to having an opportunity to be on the practice squad, to not hearing back from the Falcons, I know those ups and downs, successes and failures, and opportunities and disappointments of 1998 helped me grow stronger, but at the time, it took its toll. I wanted things to happen the way I wanted them to happen. I was still learning to trust His ways even when they weren't my own. God had a greater plan; I just couldn't see it yet.

CHAPTER 7

THE HAPPIEST PLACE ON EARTH

*"Trust in the LORD with all your heart
And do not lean on your own understanding.
In all your ways acknowledge him,
and he will make straight your paths." Proverbs 3:5-6*

(JOHN): Once the news of being cut settled, Terina and I discussed what the next step was. I decided to call my agent to give him the news since I had been speaking with him throughout the day. He told me to call him with an update as soon as I had one. When my agent picked up the phone, we talked briefly, but then he had to go. I didn't hear back from him for quite some time later, as in days later. I got my first dose of the nature of the agent/athlete relationship. In this industry, if you are on top of your game, you're the man. Once you fall, you become a nobody. In an instant, I went from being able to get in touch with him at any time to barely hearing from him at all.

While I am sure there are many great agents out there who genuinely care for their players, a fair share of them care more about what they may potentially get from their athletes than for the athletes themselves. While this was a tough lesson to learn, I learned it quickly.

(TERINA): We had no idea what to do next, so we decided to return to the West Coast. Since we weren't married yet, John went to live with his parents, and I lived with my grandparents in Chico until we knew the next step.

We planned on getting married, but with all of the uncertainties, it didn't seem like the "right time" to throw a wedding into the mix. How would we even schedule a day? We had no idea where we would be or what our schedule would look like even a week from now, let alone the next year.

There were so many unknowns at this point. I had just left school to be with him, and he had nowhere to actually be anymore. He had no idea if another team would pick him up in days, weeks, months, or not at all, which made it difficult for me to decide whether or not to go back to Nevada in the fall.

What if he did sign somewhere or if Atlanta did pick him up as they had mentioned was a possibility? If I re-enrolled at Nevada, there was a chance we would end up being apart again, and for us, that wasn't an option. We knew we were getting married, so keeping our relationship solid was more important than anything else. We decided to wait it out.

John got a job catering at a hotel and continued his training. If and when a call came, he had to be 100% in shape and ready to go at a moment's notice. There were no guarantees of getting another tryout, but he had to be ready if and when the opportunity came. He trained rigorously, ate healthy, and began working with a QB coach who helped him tremendously. Even though John felt better than ever physically, he continued to question if he was completely wasting his time. Would the call ever come, or was all of this hard work for nothing?

(JOHN): As the season progressed, it became difficult for me to even watch the NFL, as week after week and game after game went by with no call. Every time the phone rang, my heart raced: I'd wonder, if just for a second, "Is this the call I've been waiting for?" It felt like a constant letdown every time I realized it wasn't my agent calling with some good news.

Doubts began to fill my mind again as I questioned what I was doing. Was I foolish to continue to chase this dream? Was it time to move on with life, get a real job and get my head out of the clouds, as some would suggest? I became more and more unsure.

(TERINA): As the fall leaves were replaced with the sights and sounds of Christmas, John felt as though he had been waiting forever. Technically, he had. Though he spent a few months with the Dolphins, he never actually made the roster through training camp or played in a single game. His childhood dream of playing in the NFL still eluded him. All the years of perseverance and hard work still waited patiently for its reward.

(JOHN): The week before Christmas, we were visiting Disneyland with my family and had just gotten off of Splash Mountain when the long-awaited call came. A few weeks before, I had a workout with the Cleveland Browns, who were preparing to come back to Cleveland for the 1999 season and had to build a team from scratch. They hadn't hired a head coach, but the front office personnel had begun to put together a team.

My agent informed me the Browns wanted to sign me! Our day at the "Happiest Place on Earth" just became even happier. We were headed to Cleveland!

CHAPTER 8

NEW BEGINNINGS, AND A DEAD END ROAD

"No I did not injure you, but I supernaturally allowed this injury to slow you down." ~Ist Prophecy

(JOHN): As I arrived in Cleveland, it was an exciting feeling. Although the Browns were one of the oldest franchises in the NFL, they had left Cleveland for Baltimore following the 1995 season. Now they were coming back. They had the same colors and name, but everything else was brand new: they had a new owner, new coach, and a new roster. I was one of the first signees, signing even before the new head coach was announced. I knew that once the coach was signed, he could come in and release me immediately. Once they announced Chris Palmer as the head coach, my optimism definitely grew. Coach Palmer was the offensive coordinator of the Jacksonville Jaguars before accepting the position of head coach with the Browns. He was the coach who came out to Nevada to privately work me out, and the coach who had told me he wanted to draft me in the 3rd round of the draft back in Jacksonville. I just knew I had finally caught my break.

As the coaching staff was put in place, they got ready for the expansion draft and free agent signings, and then ultimately the NFL draft. Over the course of the offseason, the Browns added 6 quarterbacks to the roster. With Tim Couch the #1 overall draft pick and Ty Detmer the veteran back up, it left 4 of us fighting for two spots. We all knew the upcoming mini camps would be a battle for a position on the final training camp roster.

A few weeks before camp, we all knew that cuts were coming. I could feel the tension. Things would be different this time, however, unlike in Miami and Atlanta the year before; I was never called into the coach's office with my playbook. I was going to be one of the 4 quarterbacks on the training camp roster! Now I knew I would have an opportunity to prove myself as an NFL quarterback.

(TERINA): With all of the transitions going on, I had missed out on quite a bit of training, so I found a good swim club and began practicing and lifting weights again. In order to get to practice, I ended up purchasing a used Pontiac Sunfire, which broke down a few days after I drove it off the lot. During repairs, the dealership "generously" replaced it with a 30-year-old, dirty brown, wood-paneled, non-air conditioned, junk-mobile station wagon, which was longer than a hearse. Never mind we were dead in the middle of summer. That was just the beginning of the hilarity of this.

As shallow as it sounds, driving into John's practice facility and parking this beast was humiliating. Normally, I just deal with these things, but the irony is that growing up, my family's vehicles were legendary amongst all my high-school friends, and probably most of the town, for providing the most embarrassing and entertaining moments. My dad never spent more than $1,000 on a car, and they always had something wrong. We broke down often and ran out of gas even more often. My brother and I would try to hide every time we pulled up to school. It wasn't unusual to see my friends and me either pushing the car down the street or standing beside the car on the side of the road with the hood up, steam pouring out from the engine. For some reason, my dad loved the look of two-toned cars. Thinking it was cool, he would paint them ridiculous colors like mint and forest green, or mustard and bright yellow. We didn't find it so cool.

Throughout high school, I drove a variety of junky cars. My favorite was a large two-toned van, with a bus-sized steering wheel, a roof rack made of PVC pipe, a caved in roof, and no reverse gear. While it made parking nearly impossible, often times we couldn't park in the parking lot at all because there was no guarantee I could get out without using my reverse. When I drove my friends to the movie theater in town, we would go on a small hike. With the way the parking lot was configured, I had to park on a hill so I could coast out backwards or pull out forwards with no other cars blocking me. It also made a huge sound when starting, which only made everyone look my way. When you are trying to hide, that doesn't help. We had one car with our names spray-painted on it and another car that would stall randomly. One time while driving with a friend, the car stalled in the middle of the intersection and the horn started honking nonstop. We just died laughing. Another time, driving back from the mall with a bunch of friends, it overheated on the freeway and the engine began smoking. We veered to the side of the highway and jumped out of the car as fast as we could while my friend screamed, "It's going to explode!"

While I am thankful to have provided so much entertainment to both friends and strangers along the way, I couldn't wait for the day I would have a normal vehicle to drive. It only figured that a few days after I drove my first car off the lot, it broke down and was replaced with this piece of junk!

I decided I would wait to go to John's practice again once I got my car back. I had no idea; however, the next time I would go to the practice facility would be to drive John home.

(JOHN): While my preparation for training camp was in full swing, I had other things on my plate as well. I knew shortly after Terina and I started dating that she was the one I was going to marry, but after a few years into the relationship, I still hadn't popped the question. The day before I left for Cleveland, I bought an engagement ring, but I kept the ring "hidden," or so I thought, until I finally mustered up enough courage.

(TERINA): The funny thing about John is while he can be trusted with any secret, being able to keep any surprise "hidden" is another story. Let's just say stealth is one of the last words you would use to describe John. I was visiting John one weekend, and as we were preparing to go out to dinner one particular evening, I went to the bathroom to brush my teeth. I opened his toiletry bag on the bathroom counter to look for toothpaste when I saw *it*. A small white bag with the words "Gem Tree Jewelers" on it. I knew, if he didn't hide it, I would peek, so I calmly brought out the toiletry bag to him and asked, "Is there toothpaste in here?" He ran towards me, snatched the bag out of my hand, and stuffed it in the bottom drawer of his dresser right in front of my eyes! Well, that didn't work.

(JOHN): Honestly, I don't think I could have found a hiding place where Terina would *not* have found the ring. If Terina wants something, there is pretty much nothing that will stop her! Second, I was told by her mom she has been opening her presents in the closet and under the Christmas tree since she was barely walking. I should've known better.

(TERINA): After waiting for months, I questioned what was taking so long. The next time I was in town, I found myself down by the foot of the dresser and, with my eyes closed, pulling out the ring box, and opening it. I never peeked, but I slipped it on my finger. It fit perfectly. I hurriedly put it away, saying NOTHING to John.

At this point, I couldn't comprehend what was taking so long. By the end of a few months, I had not only slipped the ring on my finger but also had worn it to his practice. I stared at it as it dazzled in the sun while dreaming about our wedding day and what it would be like to be his wife. I couldn't stand the wait. Right before practice was over, I hurried back to his place to put it back before he got home. He never had a clue what was going on! One day, while gazing at it while I was driving, I nearly rear ended the driver ahead of me because I hadn't noticed he hit the brakes. John's delay was literally risking the lives of drivers all over the city!

(JOHN): I am still not sure why it took me so long to ask Terina to marry me. I remember times where I was so close, and then I would put it off. There was never any doubt that she was the one, but I was just scared to take the next step.

Finally, one night I mustered up the courage to do it. We went out to a nice restaurant on Lake Erie and sat at a table with an incredible view of the water. I had planned to ask Terina during dinner, but we ordered, ate, paid our bill, and I was still too nervous. We actually got up to leave when

I told Terina, "We paid a lot for the meal; let's go back to enjoy the view a bit longer." I wasn't the smoothest operator, to say the least. Once she sat back down, I began to talk about our life together, and I finally asked her to marry me. She said, "Yes!"

As we walked out of the restaurant, I was upset because I didn't even get down on one knee during the proposal. It had taken me over 4 months to get the courage to ask the question, now I had to do it twice. So out on the deck of the restaurant, I got down on one knee and asked Terina to marry me, again. I was relieved that it was over, and I couldn't wait to start our lives together.

(JOHN): It seemed as though, for the first time in a while, things were really lining up. Football was going well, we were now engaged, and Terina had started back up with swimming. I had made the camp roster and felt good about where I stood. During a conversation with Coach Palmer, he told me that, obviously, Tim and Ty would be battling for the starting job, but the 3rd spot was mine to lose. At this point in my career, sitting and learning from a #1 draft pick and a 7-year NFL veteran was the perfect situation for me.

The first day of camp was incredible. As we walked out onto the practice field for the first time, the stands at our facility were completely packed. It seemed the whole city was there. Though every practice challenged me mentally, I had physically never felt better and knew I was doing well. My confidence was back, knowing I had a good chance to make the team.

On the fourth day of training camp, I was running a play during morning practice, when I felt the outside of my left foot give out. My heart sank. I walked back to the huddle and told the guys, "I just broke my foot." I couldn't believe it. I didn't want to believe it. I actually attempted one more play, so as not to face the inevitable. I hoped my gut feeling was wrong. It wasn't, I couldn't even walk on it. As much as I wanted to push through, I had to leave practice and go to the training room. After the trainer checked my foot, he thought it was broken. He couldn't be 100% sure without an X-Ray, but I knew.

Right then I just lost it. I buried my head into a towel and sobbed. I was finally in a great situation when—BAM!—just like that, my dreams were shattered again. The X-rays confirmed a "Jones" fracture, a fracture of the 5th metatarsal bone. After consulting with the doctor, I needed to have surgery so they could insert a screw in the bone to allow it to heal properly.

(TERINA): "Terina, John's on the phone for you," my coworker said as she waved me over to the phone at the front desk. I thought, "That's strange. He never calls me while he's at practice." My heart instantly started beating through my chest and then landed in the pit of my stomach as I grabbed the receiver. I strained my ear to hear through his mumbled words, "I broke my foot."

What! What happened? I knew he wasn't joking, but I just couldn't believe it. I listened in shock as he said, "I just stepped on it." I thought quietly in a state of disbelief, *"He just stepped on it? He didn't twist it or get tackled or anything? How do you break your foot by just stepping on it?"*

I didn't ask any more questions. I left work, hopped into my extremely large station wagon, and drove to the practice facility, praying nearly the whole way there.

"Lord, what are you doing? Maybe everyone is right. Maybe this *isn't* what you have for him, *CLEARLY!* Should he go and get a *REAL JOB* like people are saying? You have shut every door so far. I can't imagine this indicating anything other than it being time to move on.

Arriving at the practice facility, I pulled up to the security gate and flashed my pass. The security guard gawked at my vehicle, trying to hide the humor he most likely found in seeing one of the player's girlfriends driving this piece of junk. As shallow as it felt in the moment, it gave me a good laugh and helped to lighten the heaviness I felt for John's injury, at least momentarily.

As I walked out onto the field, I saw John sitting on the trainer's cart with his leg propped up, wearing the most downcast look I've ever seen. He was closer than ever to his life-long dream when, once again, it was snatched out from under him. This injury would not only end his football season but also end his NFL career—at least that was what we thought. While we looked forward to the new beginning in spending our lives together, we were heartbroken that Cleveland had turned out to be a dead end road.

CHAPTER 9

GOD SAID SO

*"The Bowl is John's...If San Jose goes to the
Arena Bowl, John will be playing in it."*
~The Voice in the stands

The LORD said, "Shall I hide from Abraham what I am about to do"
~Genesis 18:17

(TERINA): After John was released from Cleveland, we headed back to Reno so that John could begin rehab on his foot. Soon after our arrival, we attended the church service where we received the 1st prophecy, the day that changed our lives forever. (See chapter 1) For the months that followed, we attempted to break it down…

*~There was a man named Jacob that I wrestled to the point that
his hip was dislocated.~*

(TERINA): We were very unclear about this. The only thing we guessed was that John was beginning or was already in his own wrestling match with the Lord.

~No I did not injure you, but I supernaturally allowed this injury to slow you down.~

(TERINA): We deliberated about from what God was slowing John down—making an NFL team, playing for the season? What? It seemed logical to assume God slowed John down from actually making the NFL and whatever would transpire from that as it seemed to be where he was headed before this injury took him out.

~I'm going to lay a foundation for a surprising success that is going to amaze you.~

(TERINA): This word gave us a sense of both excitement and wonder. I questioned what in the world could possibly happen that would surprise or amaze us at this point in our lives. We had already tasted quite a bit of "success," having both reached the highest level in our respective sports, winning championships, setting records, and receiving a lot of accolades along the way. While those were great achievements, they didn't surprise or amaze us.

The part we should've paid more attention to was the foundation-laying process we would endure prior to the amazing success that was to come. We had no idea what this process entailed.

Just like the concrete of the old foundation that is broken, crushed, split into smaller pieces, and then removed before the soil can even be prepared for a new foundation to be laid, we too would experience the same process in our lives until the previous foundation was completely crushed, broken, and ripped out of our very being. Only then He could begin preparing the ground for the new foundation He was going to lay.

~This has been the most insecure 18-month period you have ever known.~

(JOHN): The part that immediately got my attention and confirmed this was from the Lord was when I realized what took place 18 months ago. As I counted back, I realized, the first day of the NFL draft was exactly 18 months ago, to the day!
That amazed me.

~You will put up the numbers again.~

(TERINA): This part of the word was very hard to figure out. We knew it meant he would play again—hence, "putting up the numbers again"—we just didn't know where. Obviously, he couldn't go back to "put up the numbers again" at a collegiate level. The only other place where "putting up the numbers again" seemed legitimate was the NFL.

~You're going to look back and say this was the best thing that ever happened to me. ~

(JOHN): When you are coming off an injury that has basically killed your dream, these words are hard to understand. At this time, my dream was to be a NFL quarterback. Since I loved playing football and wanted to make that my career, how could getting hurt and then getting cut from the NFL be the best thing to ever happen to me? As my faith matured, however, I began to realize what God was saying. He didn't mean not playing in the NFL would be the best thing to happen to me; He meant that growing as a man of God would be the best thing to happen to me, though I didn't understand it at the time.

~The only thing worse than success is success without me, and I spared you from that.~

We could not begin to figure out what He meant by success without Him at that point in our life. Obviously, according to His word, having success *with* Him was more than simply having a relationship with Him and being successful at the same time. It would, however, take many years for us to fully understand how that was possible.

~Watch and see what I do in this hour as you follow Me. Watch and be amazed.~

(JOHN): I hadn't thought about the prophecy for a few months. I still didn't fully understand prophecy at this point and wasn't sure what to do with it. All I really thought about was football. After a few months of rehabilitating my broken foot, I was ready to play again. My agent attempted to get my name back out there to NFL teams by letting them know I was cleared to play, but I only got one workout with the Denver Broncos, though nothing came of it.

After coming off of a significant injury and having no NFL experience, it became clear teams weren't interested. While talking to my agent about other leagues, he mentioned the Arena Football League. Having seen only seen one game my whole life, I had no idea what it was about.

At this point, since my agent had basically stopped representing me,

I did some research and sent out emails to three different teams. One of those teams was the San Jose SaberCats. They contacted me to express their eagerness to bring me in for a workout. During our trip from Reno to San Diego to get married in my hometown, I stopped in San Jose for a workout. Things went well, and I signed a contract with the team. A few weeks after we got married, I headed to training camp.

During the first practice, I realized that the Arena game was a lot quicker than the outdoor game. It definitely was a learning curve for me as I barely had time to drop back before I had to get rid of the ball. The other quarterback, Mark Grieb, who had been with the SaberCats the year before, came into camp as the starter. We got along great from the very beginning. By watching him, I was able to learn quickly.

Entering the first regular season game, Mark was named the starter. We won our first game easily. I ended up getting a little playing time, which was a great way to get my feet wet in this league. The second and third games didn't go as well. We lost both games. I ended up finishing the third game and played very well. The following week the coach called me into his office to let me know I was starting the next game against the Iowa Barnstormers. It would be my first official start in a professional football game.

The game itself was a back and forth battle. Things were going well when late in the 3rd quarter, as I dropped back and threw the ball, a defensive player hit me right on my left arm with his helmet and knocked me to the ground. It was an incompletion, but that was the least of my worries. As I got up off the ground, my arm and wrist felt different. As I pushed down on my arm with my fingers, I felt the bone move. Right then I knew I had broken my arm. I couldn't believe it.

I hadn't even made it through my first professional game, when just like that, it was over. Without saying a word about my injury, I got the next play from my coach and walked into the huddle, nonchalantly stating, "I think I just broke my arm." My teammates looked at me with wide eyes as I called the play. After we broke the huddle, I walked up to the line, took the snap, and dropped back and threw a touchdown, all with a broken arm.

While everyone on the bench was celebrating the touchdown, I walked off the field knowing my season was over. My chance to prove I could play at the professional level anytime soon was over, and my chance to make it back into the NFL was over. While Terina was still in Nevada, my parents traveled to every home and away game. I waved at them to come down to the bench so I could break the news to them personally. I knew they, too, would be heartbroken.

The questions began flowing through me, "Why did this happen?" At the moment I had no answers. When I got back to San Jose, I would be heading in to my 2nd surgery in less than a year and would once again be facing an uncertain future. At this point, it clearly felt like football was not the path that God had for me. If it were, why was everything going in the wrong direction? It felt like for every step I tried to take towards my goal, I was going further away from it. I had never felt so lost and confused.

(TERINA): After watching John sit on the bench all season long with a sling on his arm, and only a few months after he recovered from his broken foot, I had major questions. As I sat in the stands watching the other quarterback play the game, I started praying about what God was doing. Through the years of setbacks, injuries, and disappointments, we were questioning everything. We were both tired of dealing with the continual trials and desperately needed some answers. Was John supposed to continue in football, or were we suffering all of this needlessly? The Bible says, "Those who chase useless dreams aren't wise." If this was a useless dream, we needed to know! It was pointless to continue pursuing something God didn't have for John.

During this time, we also had quite a few well-meaning people tell us it was obvious that God didn't want John in football and that he needed to move on with his life. Technically, it was great advice, except we had the prophetic word given to us just a few months before, which spoke of God doing something amazing with John in football, and we felt God meant the NFL in particular. Was John supposed to continue to press on? How did this prophecy apply to John's current situation, if it did at all?

As I sat in the stands, I was completely unaware of the game or of the people around me as I began pouring my heart out to God, praying and asking Him what we were supposed to do. I had never prayed before, thinking I would actually hear a response. Sure, I knew God answered prayer in a general way, but, at this point in my walk, I just didn't know prayer was a dialogue. If I listened, He would actually respond? Instead, I talked the whole time, never listening for a reply. Until this moment, I had never heard one. After I finished praying, I turned my focus back on the game, when suddenly I heard the words, "The Bowl is John's!"

"What? What was that?" I thought, both dumbfounded and in utter amazement as I repeated to myself what I had just heard. I then heard, "If San Jose goes to the Arena Bowl, John will be playing in it."

WHAT?! I literally couldn't believe my ears! Was God really speaking to me? If so, about this?

I sat there for the remainder of the game in shock, thinking about what this meant. Nothing, and I mean nothing, had ever happened like this to me before. Not only that, I had never, other than our 1st prophetic word we received a few months before, even heard of someone hearing God's voice. There was no frame of reference for this, but I knew it was real.

A surge of hope filled my heart. I wanted to immediately run down on the field to where John was sitting so I could tell him. It seemed worth getting chased down by a security guard and getting kicked out of the game if it meant I didn't have to hold in this unbelievable information a second longer.

After waiting for what seemed like years for the game to finish, I went down to the waiting area where the players' families, girlfriends, or wives waited for the players to come out of the locker room. For whatever reason, John was always one of the last ones out. Tonight, he must have taken a nap before he got dressed and came out.

"Where is he?" I questioned impatiently.

When he finally walked out of the door, I ran up to him and said, "God said the Bowl is yours!" He looked at me with this skeptical look on his face as if to say, "What in the world are you talking about?"

At this point in our lives, we had never heard God speak to us, which is why I followed with, "I know this sounds crazy, but I was sitting in the stands praying when I heard the Lord speak to me, 'The Bowl is John's,' which means if San Jose goes to the Arena Bowl, *you* will be playing in it!"

(JOHN): When Terina told me what had happened, I did not know what to think. I honestly thought she was out of her mind. What do you mean God spoke to you? If He did, why would God speak to you about football? Terina is a very passionate person, but I know for sure she doesn't lie. I had no idea exactly what to make of it. I told her we would see what happens. We both resolved to keep it to ourselves for now.

(TERINA): Neither of us knew exactly what this meant, but it was the first time in my life I knew one thing for sure—if San Jose went to the Arena Bowl, John would be playing in it! God said so!

CHAPTER 10

THERE IS A REBOUND COMING

"I even kept you from another injury that would have debilitated you. My hand of blessing is on you." ~2nd Prophecy

(JOHN): "I almost just broke my neck," I thought to myself as I quickly jumped up from the ground and grabbed the back of my neck. During the play, I had been hit from behind as I threw the ball. As my body went to the ground, face first, the front of my helmet got caught in the turf. I felt a shift in my neck. The pressure was unlike anything I had ever felt before, but suddenly, it shifted back into place. I'd been injured before and taken some hard hits in the past, but this was the scariest moment of my life. I truly believed that I had come very close to breaking my neck right there on the field in the middle of the game. I continued to play and never told anyone about it, as I knew it would just cause them to worry every game from then on.

Keep the Faith

It was my first season back with San Jose. The previous season ended with a broken arm, which resulted in surgery to place 8 screws and a metal plate in my bone. I am amazed, looking back, that I still had the determination to keep going. Entering training camp, I was named the starting quarterback. I was extremely excited to get the season started. While I knew I had a lot to prove since I only started one game the year before, it was a dream come true to have the opportunity to lead a professional football team.

We started the year off great. Heading into my most anticipated game against LA, we had the best record in the league at 5-2 and the #1 rated offense, averaging 60 points a game. I was excited. Since the game was close to my hometown of Fallbrook, many family members and friends planned on attending. The local news station also decided to do a story on me and asked if they could set up an interview with Terina during halftime. The game started off well, a back and forth battle. We weren't clicking on all cylinders but were still leading 17-14 in the second quarter. Midway through the second quarter, I dropped back to pass. The receiver had a post route, and, as he cut underneath the defender, I made my read and threw the ball. At the last minute, however, the receiver made a second move and broke over the top of the defender as the ball was in the air. The ball landed right in the hands of the defender. Interception! As a quarterback, it's frustrating when the play falls apart this way. Receivers are taught that when they make a break, stay on that angle. Unfortunately, the receiver made a second move after the ball was released, and I could do nothing but watch the ball land right into the arms of the defensive back. As I walked off the field, I didn't even have an opportunity to explain what happened to the coach. I heard the coach yell at Mark

Grieb, the previous year's starting quarterback, to get ready. Right then I knew my night was done. As Mark entered the game during the next offensive series, it was apparent to everybody in the stands that I had been benched. The interview with Terina never happened. I guess interviewing the wife of the benched quarterback doesn't make for that good of a story!

I ended up spending the rest of the season on the sidelines as I watched the team blaze their way to the playoffs again. It felt like another failed season went down into the books. It was a tough season going from starting quarterback to riding the bench. Terina and I were so happy when the season came to an end. I began again to question whether or not football was something I wanted to continue doing.

(TERINA): The morning we received the second prophecy, we almost skipped church. We were exhausted from moving from San Jose back to Reno the night before. I was six months pregnant with our 1st child, Zachary, and John had just finished another really long football season. We wanted to lie in bed and enjoy our first morning with absolutely nothing to do and nowhere to go.

Though we nearly stayed home, we finally dragged ourselves out of bed and headed to church. While we were really excited to see people we hadn't seen in a few years, we had no idea just who we were about to run into.

As we walked into the building, John nudged me and gave me this incredulous look. "He's here!" he stated emphatically. "Who's here?" I said, scanning the room, "The pastor who prophesied over us a few years ago, he's here," he said, staring towards the front of the room. I looked up and saw him. "What are the chances?" I thought to myself as my stomach filled with knots. This pastor didn't attend our church. He didn't even live in Nevada. He was visiting Reno, and it just so happened to be the very day we had come back as well.

We made our way to our seats and attempted to disappear into the crowd. While we didn't want to get called up, we somehow just knew it was happening. I looked over at John as he squirmed in his chair—he was in a full-on sweat! He looked at me with this wild look in his eyes and said, "I just know we're going up there."

It was as though something in us knew we were getting ready to hear, once again, from the Lord of Heaven and Earth. While it didn't seem as formidable as it had even a few years before, we felt a sense of reverent fear and awe.

(JOHN): During worship I kept looking over at the pastor, who seemed to be staring at me the whole time. A few rows back from him, I stood, drenched with sweat. All I wanted to do was get out of there. I knew he was going to call us up again. As soon as worship was over, he took the stage. After explaining once again what prophecy was and wasn't, he called us up to the stage and began to prophesy over us.

He started out by saying, "The moment you walked in the room, the Holy Spirit began speaking to me about you. I'm going to share it with you now."

That made sense: as the minute we walked in, we definitely felt God's presence. He continued...

"You went through a dark night. It was like a tempest. You wondered about your future, you wondered about direction, you felt like the whole bottom was falling out. For every step you tried to take uphill, it was like you were going downhill," says the Lord. It frustrated you. Just when you thought you were bottoming out, you hit bottom.

BUT YOU ARE ON THE REBOUND; there is a rebound coming. I blessed you this year, I elevated you, and you felt my grace. I even kept you from another injury that would have debilitated you. My hand of blessing is on you.

I want you to know a change is in the wind for you. You are to get ready to see me move. I'm going to bless you both in your marriage; I'm going to bless you also in the sports world. Opportunities are going to come. You're not to be afraid; you're not to worry about your future. I'm here to tell you my hand of blessing is on your life.

He finished with, "Watch and see what I do in this hour as you follow me. Watch and be amazed!"

(TERINA): Something shifted in us after receiving this prophecy. After the accuracy of this word, we could no longer question if it was from the Lord. When he spoke about "sparing John from an injury that would've debilitated him," John knew instantly what it was, though I was clueless. I figured he simply protected him from a serious injury; I didn't know John had nearly broken his neck. When he told me the full story, my arms were instantly covered in golf ball-sized goosebumps. I was incredibly humbled and grateful as I thought about how God spared him. He also spoke that we were to get ready to see Him move. A rebound was coming. It was the first time in a long time where we felt hope regarding what lay ahead in football.

(JOHN): This prophecy was huge on so many levels. To hear him say that God had spared me from another injury was one thing, but to hear the words "that would have debilitated you" completely wrecked me. I knew exactly what injury from which he spared me. When I got up after hitting my head on the ground, my first reaction was to thank God for protecting me. At that moment, all I thought was how close I was to possibly not being able to walk ever again. After hearing those words on that stage, I understood why my neck didn't keep going forward and how I was able to get up after that play. Because of God's protection, I was able to keep playing that game and was ultimately able to stand on that stage to hear God's words to me. To also know that everything I had gone through from being cut, injured, and benched was not in vain gave me a surge of strength to fight for what He still had in store for me instead of giving up. I was beginning to learn that just because we have setbacks, trials, and what seems like failure after failure, it doesn't mean God isn't with us, working for our good.

For us, it was an incredible gift to be given a prophetic word to be reminded God was with us and had a plan. Not only that, He wanted us to know about it! During a time when I personally felt like with every single step I tried to take towards my goal ended with me further from it, He had sent His word telling us we had hit bottom—but a rebound was coming!

CHAPTER 11

THE BOWL IS JOHN'S

"I have spoken, and I will bring it to pass; I have purposed, and I will do it." Isaiah 46:11b ESV

"YOU ARE ON THE REBOUND, there is a rebound coming.... I want you to know a change is in the wind for you, you are to get ready to see me move...Watch and see what I do in this hour as you follow me, watch and be amazed" ~2nd Prophecy

(TERINA): The Lord told us we were to get ready to see Him move and that a rebound was coming. Heading into the season, we knew something was about to happen; we just didn't know what, how, or when. We felt, for the first time in awhile, hope arising. It's such a dangerous thing to allow hope to creep in yet again, because hope deferred makes the heart sick. After all the continued setbacks, we were literally heart sick.

As the end of the season drew near with still no movement, we had to stand on the word we had received, knowing He would be faithful.

(JOHN): As I prepared for the 2002 football season, I truly believed something was going to happen. Heading into game #1, I knew I was going to be the backup quarterback, but I prepared myself physically as though I was the starter. However, my focus wasn't only on the field but off of the field as well. I knew my role was to focus on the players' Bible study. I worked closely with Clay Elliott, the Bay Area director for FCA (Fellowship of Christian Athletes), who had been the chaplain since I arrived in San Jose in 2000. With the SaberCats having one of the best seasons of all time and Mark having an MVP season, I continued to have peace that God was in control. San Jose was 12-0, heading toward an undefeated season, something only one other team had accomplished in the history of the Arena Football League. So far, I had only thrown 13 passes all year in mop-up duty. With only 2 games left in the regular season, during the game against the Arizona Rattlers, Mark got hit and slammed into the turf, breaking his collarbone. As I warmed up, I had mixed emotions: I was excited to get back in the game, but I felt bad for Mark. Now the team was looking at me to lead them and to continue the undefeated streak. It was a back and forth game, and it came down to the final minute. Being such a strong team, we were confident we would win. Arizona took the lead with 45 seconds left, but in the Arena Football League, that is an eternity. We drove the ball down inside the 10-yard line and faced a 4th and goal with only 2 seconds left. I felt the entire undefeated season on my shoulders. The coach called a post route to the back corner of the end zone. I dropped back and read the coverage. Our receiver beat the defender, and I made the throw for what would be the game-winning touchdown.

Was this the moment I had felt was coming? Surely something great was about to happen—God had said so! The ball was in the air for what seemed like forever. As the ball got closer to the receiver, I knew I had overthrown him. As the receiver dove for the ball, it hit his fingertips, and then bounced off the turf. Incomplete, game over! Our undefeated season was just lost. I walked off the field dejected, and, again, questioned my purpose in football.

(TERINA): I couldn't even believe it. A huge lump formed in my throat as the sting of disappointment struck me to the core yet again. "Quite the rebound," I thought to myself as my tears fell to the floor. I couldn't even begin to imagine how John must have felt to step into the starting quarterback's shoes after leading the team to an almost undefeated season. Thinking this was the moment of his redemption, he instead walks off the field coming up short in such an important game, in front of his team, coaches, fans, the media, everyone. My heart literally broke for him.

I knew he would be calling me soon, but I had no idea what to say. How could football be a part of God's plan for John's life? This whole journey so far had been in the opposite direction. It seemed ridiculous to even think there was ever a reason to have hope in a rebound coming, would that ever really happen? What possible word of encouragement could I give? At this point, my words would fall on deaf ears. Hope deferred has a way of doing that. You learn to no longer get excited or dream or hope again—you just stay neutral. Then, if things don't go as planned, you no longer feel the disappointment; it's expected. "Wouldn't it be a relief to no longer feel let down?" I thought. As the phone rang, I prayed quickly, "Lord, give me the words to say." I answered the phone with "Hello," but all I heard was an extended period of agonizing silence mixed in with muffled crying. I waited quietly, my heart physically aching in hearing his brokenness.

"Hello," I said again, waiting for words to break the silence. Right then, words invaded the conversation though they weren't John's. I suddenly heard, "You are going to play Arizona in the Arena Bowl, and you are going to win."

"What in the world?" I thought to myself, unable to believe it. Before I could even rationalize what I heard, I instantly blurted it out to John, "God just told me you're going to play Arizona in the Arena Bowl, and you're going to win!" He didn't say anything in response, so I repeated it.

"John… God literally just told me you're going to play Arizona in the Arena Bowl, and you're going to win!" I felt a surge of hope rise over me instantly, and, though nothing like this had ever happened until being in the stands a few years before, I knew it was Him. I was becoming more familiar with things involving God taking place outside my realm of limited understanding, including hearing His voice. The Bible says, "You will hear a voice behind you saying, this is the way, walk in it." (Isaiah 30:21) It was no longer simply by hearsay; I was experiencing it.

At this point, the Arena Bowl was still 5 weeks away, and there was a lot of football to be played. To make matters worse, we felt very strongly that the Lord wanted us to share this message with all the guys at the team Bible study ahead of time, before playoffs even started! I instantly panicked. "How can we possibly share something like this? What if it doesn't happen? What if God isn't saying this? They will all think I'm insane! This is wild, Lord. Are you serious?!"

After we prayed for about a week over it, we decided to break the news at the next weekly Bible study we attended at the Elliott's, who led FCA in their home. I was so nervous I thought I was going to pass out. How would I share this? It sounded ridiculous. It was only the second time I'd ever heard God speak, and I had no idea what it meant to speak it out before it happened. All I knew was the Bible verse, "And now I have told you before it takes place, so that when it does take place you may believe." John 14:29.

I knew if I waited until after it all came to pass and then said, "Oh yeah, God told me this would happen," people would think, "Yeah right!" The only way they would know it was the Lord speaking was to share it ahead of time so when it came to pass, they would believe.

When I shared the news, no one knew what to say. Everyone just looked at each other as if to say, "What does this mean?" Clay Elliot looked at me and said, "What if it doesn't happen?" I said, "I DON'T KNOW! This has never happened before." All we could do from this point forward was watch the next few weeks unfold.

(JOHN): We won our last regular season game and finished 13-1. With that record, we were the #1 seed and had home field advantage throughout the playoffs. Our first playoff game was against Tampa Bay. We trailed at halftime by only 3 points, but Tampa scored on their first drive of the second half to take an 11-point lead. Then on the next series I threw an interception, which Tampa Bay returned for a touchdown, putting them up by 18. One of my teammates looked at me and yelled, "JD!" Everyone was feeling the pressure. Our team was built for a championship, and now we were down by 3 touchdowns with only a quarter and a half to play. But I looked up to the stands where Terina was sitting, and I felt a peace I had never felt before, especially in a situation like this. After the interception, we scored 3 straight touchdowns, held Tampa Bay to a field goal, and then scored a final touchdown to take the lead for good.

We won 55-48. What a game! What a comeback!

I started to believe God's word even more. Were we really going to win the Arena Bowl, just as He had said? Now that the Tampa game was over, we still had to worry about Arizona since God said we were going to play Arizona in the Arena Bowl. The next day, Arizona played their first-round game against Carolina. As we watched the game on TV, it was the most intense game I had ever watched. So much was on the line. Arizona was ahead, but with 9 seconds left in the game, Carolina scored a touchdown to take the lead 59-55. What! How could this happen? We just told everyone that God said we would play Arizona in the Arena Bowl. How can they lose this game? What would everyone think if Arizona lost and was out of the playoffs? Terina and I looked at each other, but we didn't say a word. We just watched as God did His thing. The clock ticked down to zero, when Shredrick Bonner, Arizona's quarterback, dropped back and threw a 32-yard touchdown off the net, giving them a 61-59 victory. I have never been more excited for another team's win in my life. Arizona was still alive in the playoffs. We continued to question if this was actually happening.

When the team reported for practice a few days later, there was definitely a buzz around the locker room, particularly with the guys who knew about the word from God. While we weren't certain yet, it seemed something special was happening.

The semi-finals were against the Orlando Predators and quarterback Jay Gruden. Leading the whole game, we won 52-40, putting us into the Arena Bowl for the first time in franchise history. The team celebrated. We knew, however, that Arizona still had to win the semifinal game the next day for the word to be fulfilled. We watched in amazement as Arizona defeated Chicago the next day to set the matchup that we all knew was going to happen—San Jose SaberCats vs Arizona Rattlers in Arena Bowl 16.

We went into the game with a confidence that could only come from God. The guys in the Bible study knew we were going to win. From seeing us come back from an 18-point deficit to Arizona pulling out a stunning win with a hail-mary touchdown off the net, to each of us winning our semifinal games, we knew God was doing what He had said.

Sure enough, we won the Arena Bowl 52-14, and true to the word from God, the bowl was mine as I was named the game's MVP. As I stood on the platform receiving the trophy, everything I had gone through leading up to this moment had been forgotten. The disappointment of the draft, getting cut, injured, and benched—none of this mattered.

We were shocked at how it all happened. It's one thing to win a championship, but it's a completely different story to have God orchestrate it in such a way. Guys were in disbelief over the prophetic word coming to pass, and honestly, we were as well. We had no idea this kind of rebound was coming. It was an amazing moment!

THE CHAMPION

Arena Bowl MVP John Dutton
Was in the players' locker room
After all the celebrations
And excitement was gone.
As he sat down to take off his uniform,
He looked around
Leaned back against the wall
And smiled.
Not one teammate asked him why
He was smiling.
No one asked anything at all.
They, too, know the smile of a Champion.

~Jim Dutton, August 18, 2002

Me with my sister Janelle and family after ArenaBowl

Me with my dad & mom after ArenaBowl

CHAPTER 12

AUDIENCE OF ONE

"Remember those earlier days after you had received the light, when you stood your ground in a great contest in the face of suffering. Sometimes you were publicly exposed to insult and persecution; therefore, patient endurance is what you need now so that you will continue to do God's will. Then you will receive all that he has promised." Hebrews 10:34-36

"I'm going to give you a mantle of leadership that is not cockiness, not bravado, not mouthiness." ~2nd Prophecy

(JOHN): After the 2002 season, we moved to Southern California. I had become a free agent after the season, and some teams had begun to call me about signing with them. One day as I was leaving the gym after working out, my phone started ringing. I didn't recognize the number, but, figuring it must be a team, I answered it. "Hello," I said.

"Hi, is this John Dutton?" "Yes, it is," I said.

"This is John Elway, and..."

After he said his name, I don't have much recollection of anything else he said for a few minutes. I couldn't believe that one of the greatest quarterbacks to play the game was on the other line. John was the co-owner of the Colorado Crush, a brand-new franchise in the Arena League. After I got over the shock of talking to John Elway, we talked for a while as John explained all about the organization, the coaching staff, and their desire to sign me as their quarterback. I'd obviously heard about the Crush and Elway, but it blew my mind that John Elway wanted me to come to Colorado and lead his team. I was humbled and excited.

I couldn't wait to call Terina to tell her about the conversation. After a week or so, we decided to sign with Colorado. After the signing, the organization flew Terina and me out to Denver for a weekend where a press conference was held to introduce me and 6 other signees. I was excited for a new adventure and the chance to lead a professional team once again.

I knew there would be a lot of pressure when we reported to camp in January of 2003, but I had no idea the magnitude of it until the very first practice. As I was warming up, Elway was standing right behind me watching every throw I made. Having one of the best quarterbacks to ever play the game standing there watching you is one thing, but knowing you were the quarterback he chose to lead his team to win a championship only intensified it.

We were told by a lot of people the fans in Denver would love us if we won, but if we lost, look out. I remember thinking, "This is the Arena League, not the NFL." It couldn't be that bad. I would find out exactly what they were talking about in the weeks to come.

The Crush had put together not only a good team but also a top-notch front office and support staff. John genuinely wanted this team to be treated as a professional team, and he, of course, wanted to win. The Pepsi Center sold out for our first home game as a franchise against the Georgia Force. We jumped out to an early lead and kept it until the 4th quarter, when Georgia scored 20 unanswered points to seal the game. It was a tough loss, especially since we led most of the game.

The thing that negatively impacted the game the most was something that had never happened to me before but began happening in the 2nd half of the game. Every so often, when I would drop back to throw the ball, it would suddenly fly backwards out of my hands during the backward motion of my throw. The first time it happened, I thought it was a fluke. When it happened again, I had no idea what to do. It was embarrassing, but more importantly, it cost us the game.

This was the first time I realized how passionate the Denver fans were. I'd already felt the pressure of winning from the organization, but to hear an arena full of fans booing me was hard to handle. During the next two games, which were also at home, every so often, the ball flew backwards out of my hand, usually resulting in a turnover. While we played well, we lost both games, one with 9 seconds left and the next one in overtime. We were 0-3 at home. It wasn't quite the start we expected.

(TERINA): Every single throw became nerve-wracking as I'd stare at his arm during the backward motion, hoping it wasn't going to fly out again. With fans going crazy, yelling everything imaginable, I was trying to stay in my seat and to keep my mouth or my body from losing it on someone. I always half-joked to John that one day he was going to look up at the Jumbo Tron during the game, only to see me being hauled off by a security guard with my hands behind my back, yelling back at a fan that I would be back for him!

During one game, I called my parents and told them what was

going on. They said they would pray. About 5 minutes later, my Dad called to say, "We just prayed, and it's not going to happen again." It never did.

(JOHN): As the season went on, the losses continued to mount. With every loss, the boos would intensify and the confidence from my teammates, coaches, front office personnel, and even myself continued to fade. I began receiving a lot of criticism surrounding my manner of leadership. I was told I needed to be a more aggressive leader and even a bit cockier, even getting in guys' faces, and, if needed, cuss them out when they screwed up, amongst other things. I'm not an "in-your-face" type of guy. I worked very hard in practice, off the field in the weight room, and also in the film room. I had always believed in leading by example and being positive with my teammates. Hearing this from others caused me to believe I was clearly not a leader. Even more, I once again questioned why I was in this sport anymore.

(TERINA): Almost instantly, the relief we both felt from the brief 5 weeks of victory the previous season was *long* gone. Game after game, the fans yelled and booed at John, cussed him out, collectively chanted the back-up quarterback's name, flipped him off, not caring that his family sat right next to them. It was going to be a very long season.

While it's something fans just assume is their right, it's never easy. I guarantee they wouldn't appreciate it if I showed up to their work flipping them off, cussing them out, and chanting another employee in their company's name whom I thought could do their job much better. In any other profession, this would be completely inappropriate. For me, it was my husband's job, our livelihood depended on it, and it was hard to hear so many people yell furiously at him all season long. It wore us down beyond words.

One day, as I was emotionally exhausted, I began to pray. I grabbed the prophecy to feed on God's words: they were becoming my life. ("It is written, 'Man shall not live by bread alone, but by every word that comes from the mouth of God.'" Matthew 4:4).

As I listened to the words spoken years before, a part immediately jumped out. I heard the words, 'I'm going to give you a mantle of leadership that is not cockiness, not bravado, not mouthiness." I couldn't believe it! It applied directly to what John was going through. Even though this word was spoken years before, God had sent it ahead for us *now*, in this exact season and trial, knowing there was going to be an onslaught of opinions and accusations on a very public stage, which would cause John to question everything to the point he could no longer even see who he was. John was a leader because God had made Him to be one, not because others thought he was or wasn't. God had a plan for John in football, not based on what others thought about his ability but because God spoke it. When I shared the word with John, it helped him see how he had allowed others, instead of God's truth, define him.

(JOHN): Though the season was rough, it was the very thing God used to rip out the pieces of my old, unstable foundation, removing any part of my identity built on anything other than Him and His truth. I had based my identity on my job, my successes, what others said about me, as well as the circumstances around me. We were losing, so in my mind it meant I wasn't able to lead the team or that I wasn't good enough to play at this level. God used this season to shift my focus from just game results to what He was doing in and through me. I was learning not to play for approval of owners, fans, or teammates, but for Him alone, to play for an audience of One. It would be a very long season: going 2-14 and not winning one home game. Being booed by my own fans, my leadership ability being questioned, being benched two times throughout the year, and having the footballs fly out of my hands were difficult lessons, but what I learned from all the adversity was priceless.

(TERINA): With the AFL season over and another off-season upon us, John questioned whether or not to stay in shape. After a 2-14 season, it seemed ridiculous to "get ready" for the NFL, but he also wanted to be faithful if it was something God had for him. We discussed the 1st prophecy often, wondering what to do with it. Ultimately, after 5 years of waiting, we concluded we had it wrong and decided to forget it.

We lay in bed one night and prayed, "Lord, maybe you didn't mean the NFL, and we're okay with that. We are content here, and we lay that part to rest." Though we were genuinely happy where we were, it felt awkward speaking it out loud for the first time, because for five straight years I encouraged John to continue to train and be ready in and out of season, because we had believed it was what God meant. We said "Amen" and went to bed, but in the days that followed, something in my heart felt amiss. Had we just given up? While I couldn't shake it, I resolved at this point to move on with life and trust that if God wanted to make it clear that He in fact meant the NFL, He would.

(JOHN): A few days later, prior to the 2004 season, a buddy of mine with whom I coached called and asked if I had seen the latest issue of ESPN Magazine. I hadn't, so when I got to his classroom, he told me to open it to the first couple of pages. As I flipped through the pages, I spotted an article containing a question on the top of the page with four sports reporters answering the question. The question was, "Who will be the best QB in the NFL in 2009?" One reporter said Michael Vick, two of the reporters said Eli Manning, and the last reporter said John Dutton. I looked at it and couldn't believe it. I hadn't even gotten an NFL workout for the last 5 years and was only 1 year away from being the oldest rookie ever, so I was clearly not on anybody's radar for even the practice squad of the NFL, let alone being one of the best quarterbacks in the NFL. There were 32 starting NFL quarterbacks, 32 backups, and even more third-quarterbacks who were third string every season for the last 5 years, and I was not one of them. To pick me for this season was senseless, but to pick me 5 years from now! Comical. But for some reason, this reporter chose me.

(TERINA): When I first heard about it, my initial response was, "Wow, that's random." However, the more I thought about it, I couldn't wrap my head around what motivated the guy to pick John. It literally made no sense. Following so closely on the heels of when we had let the NFL go, we felt it was God's way of pointing us back to the original vision we had. What else could it be? So, once again, John got ready just in case an NFL team contacted him at any point during the season, but once again, it was for nothing. The NFL season came and went, and it was time to gear up for another season in the AFL,—that is, if the Crush brought him back.

(JOHN): There was a lot of uncertainty heading into the 2004 season. After going 2-14 the previous season, I honestly was surprised the team brought me back. The Colorado Crush hired Mike Dailey as their new head coach. He made it very clear to everyone on the roster that all positions were up for grabs, especially the quarterback position. We had recently found out Terina was pregnant with our second child,

Drew, and providing for our growing family added to the pressure of making the team. I battled my way through camp against some tough competition; I earned the starting job heading into week 1. I knew, though, that things would have to go much differently from the year before, or I would be gone.

With the first game of the season at home, I felt we owed it to the fans to bring a victory home as we didn't win a single home game the season before. We held a 10-point lead heading into the 4th quarter, but after a fumbled snap, the Las Vegas Gladiators scored 21 points in a row to take an 11-point lead with less than a minute to go in the game. I came off the field and sat on the bench, knowing that my career—not only in Colorado but also in football entirely—was possibly over. I was *done*! My good friend and teammate, Ahmad Hawkins, who was sitting next to me, heard me say, "I am done playing football. I'm hanging up my cleats." Hawk looked at me and said, "You're not done yet; God has a plan for you in football. Don't give up now. You're playing for Him, for an Audience of One."

I instantly felt a renewed sense of strength. I didn't realize how much I would draw from those words in the years to come. Every time I felt like quitting, I would remember Hawk's words or hear them from Terina. It gave me strength to continue. It wasn't about me or my career—it was about Him.

With less than 30 seconds left in the game, I walked out onto the field, having no idea what to expect. We ran a few plays, and then with 12 seconds left, I threw a touchdown to come within 5 points. We went for the onside kick and recovered it. With 4 seconds left on the clock, Damien Harrell went long, and I threw the ball down the field to go for the win. It seemed as the though the ball hung, suspended in the air, for an eternity, as players on both teams scrambled downfield hoping for the grab, until Damien came down with the game-winning touchdown.

It was an unbelievable finish. I have won championships and other big games, but game 1 of the 2004 season was the highlight of my career. In the Arena League, crazy things like this happen, but this was special. I knew God was confirming to me that day, "I'm not done with you in football."

It continued to serve as a reminder my life wasn't about anything other than Him. My role was not to try to win games for myself or for others; my role was to please Him, trust Him through the ups and downs, and remember to do everything for an Audience of One.

CHAPTER 13

AND YOU'RE GOING TO WIN

*"So do not throw away your confidence; it holds a great reward.
You need to persevere, so that after you have done God's will,
you will receive what He has promised."*
1 Corinthians 15:58 NIV

"You are going to play San Jose and Chicago in playoffs and win."
~ The Voice in the stands

(TERINA): Of all the places God could choose to show up and speak, the football arena seemed to be the place where the most amazing things would continue to happen. It surprised me even more that football seemed to be the topic of choice. Apparently, God enjoys talking sports!

It had been a few years since I had heard His voice for the first time in the stands. As unusual as it was, I figured it was a one-time thing. But as I sat in the arena during a blowout loss against San Jose in 2005, I suddenly heard the Lord say, "You are going to play San Jose and Chicago in the playoffs and win." I was shocked and thought to myself, "Is this happening again? God, is that you?"

Before I even had a chance to fully process what I was hearing, Shalon Baker, a former teammate of John's from San Jose, walked up to me after the game to say hi. He was one of the players who attended the Bible study in San Jose, and he was present when John and I shared the prophetic word and then witnessed its fulfillment at the Arena Bowl. As he walked up to me, he said, "I hope things don't continue to go this rough for you guys," jokingly rubbing in their victory.

Without thinking, I responded, "I don't know. God is speaking to me again as he did in San Jose. I think He's getting ready to do something big again. I think we might be seeing you in playoffs." He looked at me, curiously, saying, "Hmmm...We'll see!"

After I spoke those words, I was instantly filled with faith. I couldn't wait to share with John God's newest prophetic words.

(JOHN): We had just got beaten pretty badly by San Jose when Terina came up to me to tell me that God had spoken to her: We were going to play San Jose and Chicago in the playoffs, and we were going to win. Are you kidding me? Is this happening again?

At this time, we still had 4 games left in the regular season and had not clinched a playoff spot; neither had San Jose or Chicago. While it sounded crazy, after experiencing what God did in 2002, it was not hard to believe her. After discussing it, we began to feel, once again, God wanted us to share it with the Bible study. In Colorado we had a strong team of believers, so the study was made up not only of players but also coaches and front office personnel. It was going to be a much different situation telling all of them. Terina and I took a step of faith in 2002 by telling a handful of players, but this time, the whole organization would find out.

When the day of the Bible study arrived, I sat in the back, nervous, even sweating, waiting for the chance to share. As I asked if I could say something, I looked around the room to see players, coaches, and front office personnel looking at me. I said, "This is going to sound crazy because, honestly, it is." I gave them a little background about what God had spoken to Terina in 2002 and shared the story about how it came to pass. Then I told them God had spoken to Terina again, telling her that first we would play San Jose and Chicago in the playoffs and then win the Arena Bowl. I had no idea what everyone was thinking as they looked at me, but I couldn't help but think about what they would think of me if it didn't happen. After I finished talking, my head coach, Mike Dailey, looked at me and said enthusiastically, "I love it. Let's go!"

In the weeks that followed, people who weren't in the Bible study, being intrigued, asked me what God had said. It gave me an opportunity to share the story and leave the rest in God's hands. We definitely held nothing back; we trusted that God would do what He had spoken.

For the rest of the season, we prayed like never before and watched the scores continually to see God's words unfold. On one hand, we knew it was going to happen. Yet, remaining unwavering was difficult as doubts and fear would creep in. We questioned, "What if it doesn't happen? What if it wasn't God? Will everyone think we are insane?"

We ended up finishing the season with a 10-6 record, winning our conference, giving us the #1 seed. San Jose lost 3 of their last 4 games and made it into the playoffs as the #4 seed. Chicago ended with the same record but beat San Jose in the regular season which gave them the #2 seed. With that, the first round matchup was set: Chicago vs. Los Angeles and *Colorado vs. San Jose*. Just as God had said.

As we prepared for San Jose, a lot of buzz surrounded the team, not only because it was playoffs but also because of the prophecy. During Bible study, we discussed, with a victory, that we would not take the glory ourselves. If He was orchestrating all of this, we couldn't take the credit. And we asked ourselves if God could trust us with this victory?

Now, all we had to do was go out and beat San Jose. This was not an easy matchup. Since 2003, Colorado had lost all four games to San Jose by an average of 30 points. We hadn't simply lost; we were blown out every single time. As the game started, I felt a sense of peace that I hadn't felt since the 2002 playoffs. While my faith had grown immensely because of that year, I still had anxiety once Terina and I, once again, revealed the prophecy.

We opened the game by returning a kickoff for a touchdown and never gave the lead back, winning the game 56-48. After the game, Shalon Baker came up to Terina and said, "I guess you were right—God is up to something!" At this point, we both knew He was right. God surely was.

Throughout our game, the announcers would share updates on the other playoff games. When they announced Chicago was down by 14 points in the 4th quarter, I got a little nervous. A short time later, however, the final score was announced; Chicago had scored 21 unanswered points in the 4th quarter to pull out a 7-point victory. Their victory set up a semifinal matchup with us. Unbelievable!

(TERINA): The Chicago game, notoriously called the Confetti Game, was one of the most intense games I've ever witnessed. Not only was qualifying for the Arena Bowl on the line but also validating the truth of the prophetic word.

(JOHN): We took a commanding 20-point lead in the 2nd quarter, only to see it fade away in the 3rd. The 4th quarter was a back and forth battle with us taking the lead with just under 3 minutes to play. On the final play in regulation, Chicago threw the ball for the game winning touchdown, but our DB, Rashad Floyd, intercepted the pass as the clock ran out. Confetti was blasted onto the field from both end zones, signaling a Crush victory. This celebration quickly came to a halt when everyone finally saw a penalty flag lying on the turf. We had been called for defensive pass interference. With 0 seconds left on the clock, Chicago kicked a field goal, taking the game into overtime. The "Confetti Game" was delayed for nearly 15 minutes while they attempted to remove the confetti from the field. We got the ball first in overtime, but I ended up throwing an interception. I couldn't believe it. All Chicago had to do was get a field goal to end the game. After all of this, it couldn't possibly end this way!

With the ball in their hands and the game on the line, Chicago faced a 4th down and went for a short 35-yard field goal to give them the victory. I couldn't watch the kick as I sat breathless on the bench. The ball was snapped, the holder put it down on the turf, and the ball sailed in the air—just right of the goal post. No good! We took over possession of the ball. A few plays later, I threw a touchdown pass, but another flag resulted on the play. We waited anxiously to hear the ruling. The flag was on Chicago! Touchdown, Colorado Crush! The game was over. WE WON!

It was unbelievable. So many players, friends, staff, and even personnel came up to us, absolutely amazed at what had happened, giving God the glory. One member of the front office staff came up to Terina and said, "I can't believe God just did that. I have the biggest goosebumps ever!" We all did!

We ended up going to the Arena Bowl and winning the Championship for the 2nd time in my career. It was an amazing moment for our family and the whole organization. To go from 2-14 just two years before to hoisting the Jim Foster Trophy as Arena Bowl Champions was an amazing feat. To see God work was even more amazing. After the game, God got all the glory. Yes, we celebrated on the field and in the locker room. Yes, we had a parade and a ring ceremony. But it was not your normal championship; we had trusted God enough to tell everyone we knew.

God's word says, "I tell you these things before they take place so that when they do, you will believe!" (John 13:19) He also says, "Surely, the Sovereign Lord does nothing without revealing His plans to His servants, the prophets." (Amos 3:7)

While we weren't sure why He chose to move this way, we do know it caused quite a few guys to think about God, prophecy, and His sovereign hand, causing them to believe not only that He knew the future but also that He was involved and sovereign of the affairs of men.

There were definitely tough times over the course of the first 3 seasons in Colorado. From going 2-14 in '03, to getting booed and benched, to walking off the field in '04 wanting to quit, and to going through losing streaks, there were times I couldn't wait for the season—and sometimes my career—to be over. There also were great moments as well. Winning on a last second pass against Las Vegas, having the biggest turnaround in Arena Football league history, and ultimately winning a championship taught me about perseverance, endurance, and God's faithfulness. The lessons I learned throughout those years strengthened me for what was to come. At the time, I thought these lessons were only for the football field. Little did I know He was preparing me for a much different field, a field halfway around the world.

CHAPTER 14

FIELDS OF
THE FATHERLESS

"Religion that God our father accepts as pure and faultless is this, to look after orphans & widows" James 1:27a

"John Dutton landed in Ethiopia in 2006 as a star Arena Football League quarterback. Then he stepped off the plane..."
~*San Antonio Express Newspaper*

(JOHN): Often times, when people think of Ethiopia, they recall images of starving children, nameless and faceless, published during the severe famine in the 80's. It was the worst famine the country had experienced in over a century. Stories of unimaginable suffering emerged worldwide, though they often times fell on indifferent ears. It was this "field" God had in mind when we started our non-profit in 2005, just a few months after the Arena Bowl. Being open to anything God had for us, we prayed,

"God, this is yours. Show us what to do and where to go." This prayer would lead us to an orphanage there less than 6 months later.

It started with one of my wife's many *wild ideas*: to go to Africa, a land for which she had always had a heart. While I had never thought of going to any third-world country, I did remember back in 2001 hearing about a member at our church who had started an orphanage in Africa.

When he talked about the kids and his experiences over there, I was intrigued. God was planting a seed even back then, though I had no idea. Our church in Colorado was very active in missions around the world. One day following church, Terina spoke with the missions pastor to get information on their projects and set up a meeting. I should've known better than to send her alone, but God knew exactly what He was doing.

(TERINA): Prior to meeting with the missions pastor, I sat in the car and prayed, "Lord, if there is something you want us to be a part of, let it jump out at me." We were open to whatever He had but needed Him to make it clear. During our meeting, we discussed ministries with whom they were partnered, but I wasn't drawn to anything he showed me. As I got up to leave, I saw a screen saver picturing a group of children, which immediately caught my attention. The pictures leapt off the screen as though they were being highlighted for me. Enthusiastically, I said, "Where is that? Tell me about this?" It was an orphanage in Ethiopia he had visited just a week before. He expressed the need for people to travel there to do a needs assessment so that they could move forward. Knowing instantly this was God's leading, I blurted out, "We'll go!" That was it.

(JOHN): I really didn't think about what might come from Terina's meeting. But if you know Terina, anything is possible. Terina came home and said, "Well, John, I think the ministry may be starting in Ethiopia, and we need to go this summer. What do you think?" She was asking what I thought, but she had already volunteered us. Neither of us knew this meeting would start us on the journey of our lives. If you would have told us at this point in our lives, that one day we would give up our lives, a paycheck, comfort, security, and safety to serve and even live overseas, adopting multiple children, and be involved in full-time ministry, we would've laughed in your face. But, we were committed to Terina's crazy idea, and we started planning our trip to Ethiopia.

(TERINA): When we first stepped off the plane, the guards walking around the airport with machine guns immediately startled me. "That's welcoming!" I thought to myself sarcastically. We collected our bags, mostly full of donations, and headed towards the exit. We noticed officials at the baggage claim exit scanning every bag before letting anyone leave the airport. We anxiously awaited our turn, and, as they scanned our bags, they questioned us about everything inside. "What are these for? Why are you bringing this? Are you going to sell this stuff? Who are you giving this to?" We would later learn that bag or item confiscations and bribes were a somewhat common occurrence, though we were spared the hassle on this trip.

We had no idea who the person was picking us up, nor did we have a phone, so we scanned the crowd for someone who looked like they expected us. We were so naïve! Once we found our host for the trip, we walked out of the airport, and what seemed like a million people ran up to us, hoping that we would hire them to carry our bags. Our host yelled at them, shooing them away.

Once out of the airport, the sights, smells, and the surroundings were so foreign, yet strangely familiar, like home. Little did I know two of my children were already living in this country, and this first trip brought us one step closer to bringing us together. I had no idea our family, one day soon, would call this land home off and on for years, but for now, we were simply visiting for a week, nothing more.

As we drove away from the airport, I panicked momentarily: "OH MY WORD, I am in *Africa!*" I thought. As we drove across the city to our guesthouse, I kept repeating to myself, "Oh MY WORD, I'm in *Africa. What* am I doing here? How did this happen?" My anxiety increased, most likely in response to our driver nearly running over a man lying on the highway whose legs were sticking out into the road as cars simply drove around him like it was normal. I asked, "Is someone going to run over his legs?" and the driver nonchalantly replied, "Probably," as he maneuvered the car around him, not slowing down at all. If it wasn't that, it may have been the at least 10 near-death experiences we had driving in the span of about 5 minutes as we weaved in and out of non-existent lanes dodging goats, donkeys, chickens, stray dogs, herds of cows, pedestrians, other cars, taxis, naked people, and any and everything else you could possibly imagine on the "highway." I've never, up to this point, had my life flash before my eyes as many times as it did in that small amount of time. "I will surely die on this trip!" I thought to myself half-jokingly, before my gaze was suddenly struck with something else.

POVERTY.

I'd tried to prepare myself for the trip by imagining what it would be like to experience poverty firsthand instead of merely in pictures, but no words exist to describe how you *feel* when you are exposed to it in this magnitude personally for the first time. We were stunned! It was raining, and mud was everywhere—muddy roads, muddy side streets flowing with water mixed with sewage, and muddy footprints left from the children who ran around bare-footed. This muddy stream of contaminated water flowed into some of the small shacks that lined the alleys and byways, turning their dirt floors into pools of mud. I was so overwhelmed.

(JOHN): During the drive to our guesthouse, I was overwhelmed by the poverty I saw. We saw families of 6 or more living in no more than 10x10 spaces. These "homes" were small square huts made of dried mud and tarps or metal sheets for the roof. There was no running water or sewage. After seeing homeless people, even young children, lying on the sidewalks with ripped up clothes, I realized the people with any form of shelter, even the small mud huts, were the fortunate ones. People dug in the trash for food, and street kids ran up to our window begging for money so they could eat. "Where did all these kids come from? Who is caring for them?" I thought. We learned later, many of them are owned by pimps who make them beg, only to take all the money for themselves. Their eyes would pierce me as they would motion to their stomach with a look of despair, as if to say, "I am *so* hungry. Please help me." We saw people who were crippled lying on the streets throughout the city. One young man wore shoes on his hands, using them to drag his crippled body around the middle of the road. His clothes were filthy and shredded, and he had no way of getting off the muddy ground on which he pulled his limp body around. "Was there nowhere for him to go but out on the streets, in the rain?" I kept thinking.

(TERINA): As we arrived at the Guesthouse and were escorted to our room, I've never been more eager to shut the door behind me and crawl into bed. It was difficult to fully face the reality of what people were experiencing. Was it only a mere hour ago that my little bubble still existed? I was already overwhelmed, and I hadn't even gone anywhere yet!

The next day we headed to the orphanage, a few bumpy hours out of the capital, though it felt like a world away. We saw small mud huts tucked away in the hills, smoke rising from thatched roofs made of palm trees and banana leaves. We saw men plowing the fields with their oxen, ladies lugging water on their heads or massive bundles of sticks on their backs, donkeys hauling enormous bales of hay, and children running around without shoes, and some without clothes. It was like we had been planted in an episode of the National Geographic.

When we pulled up to the orphanage where we would spend the next 7 days, we glanced at each other with a look, as if to say, "What were we thinking? Are we *really* doing this right now?" There was no running water, no flushing toilet, no hot showers, no phone, no internet, and not a single person who spoke English. Our English-Amharic translation book would be our only communication tool for the next week.

As we hopped out of the car, I saw a horse cart run by. It was made of rickety wood, covered in mud, and nearly falling apart. If we decided to go anywhere outside the 4 walls of the orphanage, that would be our mode of transportation.

We grabbed our bags and headed for the gate. At this point, we had no idea our lives were about to change, literally, forever. We were to discover the very purpose for which God had us on this earth, and to meet Mikias, a boy who would, less than a year later, become our son through adoption.

(JOHN): The minute they opened the gate, a small group of children came running up to us, laughing, squealing, hugging and kissing us all over our faces. It was as if they had known us our whole lives. In that instant, we were overwhelmed with love and compassion for these children. We felt a wave of excitement come over us.

As we sat down for our first lunch in the orphanage, I got a sense of how Buddy felt in the movie Elf. The table and chairs were the size of our kindergarten ones in America, and, being 6'4", I am sure I gave everyone some entertainment. The kids sat at another table quietly eating, but I would look over and catch them all staring and giggling at us while whispering amongst each other.

(TERINA): It was quite the adjustment. First, we had to get used to having no running water. Then we had to get used to eating our meals from the food plucked right out of the garden, the same garden the pit latrine overflowed into because of the rains. This made me contemplate fasting for the rest of the trip. I literally had to pray for the ability to withhold my gag reflex every meal. The funniest part was every time either of us finished our last bite, the cook, who treasured cooking for us and was an amazing hostess, would plop another huge portion onto our plates and say, "Bila," which meant "Eat!" It was considered rude to not do exactly that. I ended up sneaking food onto John's plate every chance I got!

Our first time in Ethiopia

And just when my gag reflex had exhausted itself, I decided it was a good idea to take a breather and politely excuse myself for a bathroom break. I asked where the bathroom was located and walked out of the dining room thinking I could take a breather when, from 100ft away, I caught the scent no words could effectively describe. I knew it was emanating from the toilet and immediately decided holding my breath was a much better option. The bathroom ended up being a drop-in toilet that overflowed because of the rain, making standing in the overflow unavoidable. The hole had maggots, and flies were everywhere on the warmer days. No pumps were available to clean it out, and there were no chemicals to get rid of the smell. I would attempt to finish and leave without taking a breath or passing out. It was quite the experience for us spoiled Americans.

(JOHN): Throughout the week, Terina and I spent most of our time living life with the kids and staff, playing and eating together. As we began to hear the stories of each child, God began to break our hearts for the things that broke His. Many of them had lost their parents or had been left at the orphanage because their moms couldn't afford to keep them. One child had been found nursing on her deceased mom. Another child had been thrown into a field a few hours after he was born and was discovered later, lying next to the headless body of another baby, most likely eaten by wild animals. It was unimaginable. I knew immediately no child should endure this, and something must be done.

At one point, I asked Miki, now our son, what God meant to him. He replied, "He is my Father. My earthly father died, but when I came here, they taught me that I still have a Father in Heaven who loves and knows me."

John and Miki

They recognized God had saved their lives by bringing them to this place and felt honored He would be their dad and call them by name. Their understanding of this showed in worship, which they did for at least an hour every morning, often with tears, and hands raised high in genuine praise. We heard comments like, "Even if we don't eat today, we will wake up tomorrow, because He sustains us." My faith felt stale, apathetic, and ungrateful in comparison.

As our trip came to an end, I knew my life would never be the same. A saying goes, "I need Africa more than Africa needs me." It's definitely true! Yes, we can make a significant difference in their lives, but the strength, perseverance, faith, and love-filled friends we met made just as much of a significant difference in our lives as well. To see them so full of joy, and praising God wholeheartedly in spite of their situation, challenged me. We can all learn from that.

(TERINA): Upon returning to the states, we saw life through a completely different lens. For the first time, we saw clearly how our house, possessions, income, and abundance had become too much of a priority. Though we were tithing, we realized that in light of their complete lack of basic necessities, we could no longer justify our spending the way we used to. We began seeing scripture differently as God opened our eyes to verses like, "I am generous to you *so that* you can be generous to others," and "I will make of you a great nation, and I will bless you and make your name great, *so that* you will be a blessing." (Genesis 12:2) It challenged us to see everything we had received from Him as a gift entrusted *to* us, not only *for* us, because loving our neighbors *as* ourselves meant we became *as* concerned for those He placed before us as we were for ourselves.

We studied the scriptures, researching the hundreds of Bible verses about being His hands and feet to the orphaned, widowed, poor, and broken in our world. We discovered, according to verses like James 1:27 and Jeremiah 22:16, that caring for orphans, widows, the poor, and the needy wasn't a calling—it was a definition of what it meant to be one who knows God.

This "wild idea" of mine profoundly changed us forever. Prior to this trip, we sponsored kids, tithed, and volunteered in the community, but this was different. Until now we had never *felt* God's heart for others in a way that broke ours. We had never *felt* the kind of compassion that made us both want to sell everything we possessed and give it away, the kind of compassion that resulted in action, where we could no longer be satisfied with giving and serving in a way that cost us little to nothing. We could no longer justify half-hearted giving, only after the needs of our family were met.

In Ethiopia, hospitality is an important part of their culture, even when it costs them tremendously. We went to an area where young girls were being sold at night to provide food for their family. Since we had eaten lunch prior to arriving, the villagers were told not to prepare food for us in order to save the little food they had. But when we arrived, a meal of boiled potatoes, bread, and soda awaited us. We had no other choice but to accept the meal so as not to be rude. We discovered afterwards, many families wouldn't eat for days because of the meal they prepared for us. Drinking a soda purchased by them, knowing it was a luxury enjoyed maybe twice a year on special holidays, left me speechless. I couldn't grasp that kind of sacrifice.

(JOHN): In Africa, everything changes—who you are, what's important, what's the definition of success, and why we're given success in the first place. Sure, in America I was a professional quarterback, but in Africa, it felt shallow to think that position mattered at all. In this moment, nothing mattered except what I could do to alleviate the suffering in front of me. Whatever lack they had physically was nothing in comparison to what we lacked spiritually. The abundance of our lives robbed us of the deep level of faith, trust, and dependence on the Lord that Ethiopian people walked in minute by minute.

After returning home, we immediately launched our ministry. We also began the process of adopting Miki, the oldest boy in the orphanage, whom God had put on our hearts while there. He joined our family about a year later. I always had felt my life's purpose was on the football field. I never realized God had a much more significant field in mind—the fields where His treasure lies, the fields of the fatherless.

CHAPTER 15

THE WORD TESTED US

"He had sent a man ahead of them, Joseph, who was sold as a slave. His feet were hurt with fetters; his neck was put in a collar of iron; until what He had said came to pass, the WORD of the Lord tested Him." Psalms 105:19

"The Kingdom of Heaven is like a treasure that a man discovered hidden in a field. In his excitement, he hid it again and sold everything he owned to get enough money to buy the field." Matthew 13:44

(TERINA): I stared out the window of the airplane, reflecting on my trip to Ethiopia over the last 10 days. I couldn't shake the feeling that God had more for us there. Did He want us to move there for a longer period of time? I knew John was beginning to feel the same way, but I questioned how it would work if John was still playing football and if the

1st prophecy was to direct our next steps in any way. It had been 10 years since we had received the 1st prophecy in 1999, and we were still waiting on the central piece to come to pass. Initially, we were pretty confident God meant the NFL with the first prophecy; however, after years of waiting, we were convinced we had it wrong, and quite honestly, we were okay with that.

It had been 5 years since the ESPN magazine article came out and a decade since the original prophecy, and I deeply questioned if the ESPN magazine was enough to stand on in regard to believing John was going back to the NFL.

I was on my way home from a trip to Ethiopia when I leaned my head against the window and prayed about the Promise. Was everything a big coincidence? With the many incredible things that happened over the course of John's AFL career, it seemed plausible to assume He meant the AFL. If God wanted us to believe specifically for the NFL, I needed a concrete confirmation.

Before I landed, I prayed, "Okay, God, we're at a crossroads. If John retires, we'll have more time for our ministry, but if you mean the NFL, we need a specific confirmation. If nothing happens, I will take it as a "no" and then we can move on and consider what being involved in Africa more would look like.

The next morning, as I was sitting in bed recovering from jet lag, John came in and said, "Kind of strange, Kyle Moore-Brown just called me to tell me he was watching NFL Today, and the announcers were talking about what 2 quarterbacks could come in right now and make a difference. They mentioned me!"

Why did it always surprise me when God did something like this? "Are you serious?" I responded. "You have no idea how wild that is!" I said excitedly and proceeded to tell him how I'd prayed for God to confirm if He was still asking us to believe in the NFL. Once again, He did.

John trained the entire fall season, as we watched and waited, hoping this would finally be the year. As weeks went by and another season passed, we felt the disappointment of another year gone by, knowing it meant we'd have to do this all over again. How much longer, Lord? I'll never forget the night the Super Bowl was over, indicating another season ended. After everyone was asleep, I dropped to the floor in exasperation. How could we keep going like this?

Believing God became the ultimate battle of faith. Everything in us was ready to move on. We were perfectly content without the NFL. Our hearts were drawn to serving our ministry full time and making a difference in the lives of others, not climbing the proverbial ladder of success simply to achieve it. We desired to find the purpose He had for us. If He was asking us to believe His word to us, we didn't want to waver in faith, which became the biggest test of all.

I related to the Bible verse in Psalm 105:17-19 regarding Joseph, where it says, "...he had sent a man ahead of them, Joseph, who was sold as a slave. His feet were hurt with fetters; his neck was put in a collar of iron; until what He had said came to pass, *the WORD of the Lord tested Him.*"

In the story of Joseph, he had a dream of 11 sheaves of wheat (representing his 11 brothers) bowing down to him. He then had another dream of the sun, moon, and 11 stars bowing down to him. However, long before the dream was ever fulfilled, Joseph's brothers sold him as a slave. He was taken to Egypt where he's falsely accused and thrown in prison. At this point, holding onto the promise God gave him seemed irrational as he sat falsely imprisoned in a foreign land, being sold by the very ones who had bowed to him in the dream.

In the devotional *Streams in the Desert*, it says:

"Think, for example, of Joseph, whom the Lord was training for the throne of Egypt. Psalm 105:19 says; 'The word of the LORD tried him.' It was not the prison life with its hard beds or poor food that tried him but the word of the LORD. The words God spoke into his heart in his early years concerning his elevated place of honor above his brothers were the words that were always before him. He remained alone in prison, in spite of his innocence. Yet, he remembered God's words *even when every step made fulfillment seem more and more impossible.*"

~Mrs. Charles Cowman

For us, this rang true. To have so much time go by with no fulfillment tested our faith beyond measure. I recalled the confirmation from 2004 about the 2009 season and resolved to forget it forever if it didn't happen by then.

During this same season of our lives, God began drastically shifting our perspective, thanks to Africa. It started with another word He used to test us in Matthew 19:21: "If you want to be perfect, go and sell all your possessions and give the money to the poor, and you will have treasure in heaven. Then come, follow me." We felt God asking us to do just that—were we willing? At first, we decided to downsize and found a house half the size of our current home. We prayed for the Lord to shut the door if owning a home wasn't what He had for us. On the day we went to put a down payment on it, someone showed up before us and outright bought it with cash! "Does that even happen, ever?" I said to John in complete shock. Only to us! God was making it clear—He wanted us to sell everything and give to the poor.

This word tested us! While it was easy to read about and discuss, when it came time to actually do it, it was difficult. God used a visiting pastor from Ethiopia to erase any remaining hesitation entirely. When I found out he was coming to visit us, I seriously contemplated borrowing a friend's house to host him since it felt absolutely ridiculous to live in a house big enough to house 50 orphans for just the 5 of us. Seeing the pastor's reaction when he walked into our more-than-adequate home only confirmed what I felt. We no longer felt comfortable living with so much excess. Though our house was a basic, upgraded tract home, it was time to sell!

The initial stage of selling things off wasn't too challenging, but the last time I walked out the door of my nest and the consistency, comfort, and security it provided and left it all behind, it was *hard*. It truly opened our eyes to how entangled we were by it.

On one hand, we were eager and full of joy, focused on what lied ahead with our ministry, but there were moments where choosing to lay down all of our earthly possessions was painful as well. We ultimately decided the Colorado Crush team housing was perfect for our family. What else did we need? It was a 3-bedroom apartment, and our younger boys could share a room.

During the offseason, we drove West to California with 1 bag each and lived there for 4 months while John coached at the Community College. We slept on blow-up mattresses and found furniture at garage sales or through friends. We were quickly becoming accustomed to living with less. Though we didn't know it at the time, it was just the beginning of becoming accustomed to living on less. Just ahead, John would get a call that would change the next 9 years of our lives significantly. Another word would test us this time as He'd challenge us to walk away from everything, removing anything we didn't choose to leave behind.

CHAPTER 16

ENTANGLED

"let us throw off everything that hinders and the sin that so easily entangles. And let us run with perseverance the race marked out for us" Hebrews 12:1

"the Lord sends poverty and wealth; he humbles and exalts. He raises the poor from the dust and the needy from the ash heap." 1 Samuel 2:7

(JOHN): After the 2008 season, we heard rumors of some owners wanting to shut down the Arena League. Since we were in California where I spent my offseason coaching at College of the Siskiyou's, all we could do was wait to see if the rumors were true. We had become good at waiting. In December, I went on a trip to Uganda for our ministry. While there, my teammate informed me that the 2009 season had been cancelled. Being in Africa, losing my job didn't hit me so hard, but, when I got back to the states, it hit me like a ton of bricks. In an instant, I lost my job, our housing, and health insurance for our entire family. We were also in the beginning process of adopting another child from Africa but could no longer move forward as we didn't have a home, income, or anything. Imagining him having to sit there and wait in an African orphanage for who knew how long was gut-wrenching. This loss affected us personally and our ministry. Our main fundraiser of the year was JD's Touchdown Club, where I raised money for every touchdown I threw. If there was no season, our biggest fundraiser of the year was down the drain as well. We lost it all with one phone call.

(TERINA): Prior to the housing market crash, our house was up for sale, but we hadn't found a buyer. When the housing market began its drastic downward spiral, we lost significant money in our home. At one point, our house had lost so much equity we would've owed $80,000 *after* selling it. We had put that much down as a cash deposit! Our payment was also about to double because we couldn't get our appraisal back at what we needed. Our backup plan of renting our house was no longer an option. Though we had found a renter, we would have to charge double just to make the payment. The potential renters actually accused us of not renting to them because they were a multiracial family. I questioned if they had seen the pictures on my wall of our multiracial family, with our African-American son right in the middle. Clearly that wasn't the reason! Regardless, like so many others during the collapse, we ended up losing our home.

Once the league was suspended, we lost everything else over the course of the next 18 months, as we were forced to deplete both our savings and our 401(k) just to get by. Things were deteriorating so rapidly I couldn't even process it.

In the midst of everything, we had to move out of the house we were living in while John was coaching.

Now what?

Our backs were against the wall, and we desperately needed God's provision for housing immediately. While we searched for a place, we went from hotel rooms, to our friends' homes, to my parents, to a small apartment above a barn—a literal red barn with hay and tractors underneath! What was happening to our lives?

We ended up meeting a missionary couple who were moving to Nepal in 3 weeks and needed someone to live in their house while they were away, rent free, in exchange for keeping up the place. What an answer to prayer!

We had to wait 3 weeks until they left, so we again went from hotels, to friends' homes, to anywhere else we could sleep. I'll never forget moving back into the hotel for a few days and setting up "home" there for the second time. John looked at me as we walked in and said, "Look at the bright side. We have a big backyard for the kids and a Jacuzzi," referring to the area out back of the hotel and the disgusting Jacuzzi down the hall. I half laughed and half wanted to cry.

We stacked groceries by the door in our makeshift pantry. I prepared dinners like peanut butter and jelly sandwiches or rotisserie chicken from the store. There weren't enough beds for all of us, so the kids took turns sleeping on the floor. It didn't help when I had the flu, and two of the kids got pink eye. I thought I was going to lose it.

At one point during this three-week waiting period, our firefighter friends had to report to a fire and let us stay in their house for a few days. We loaded up our stuff and moved in. It was so crazy during this time that I practically had no idea what month it was.

One night I sat down on the couch to read a marriage magazine after putting the kids to bed. On the front cover were the words, "Ways to Celebrate Your Marriage All Year Long." John and I had a running joke about how often to celebrate anniversaries. When we first dated, he gave me a card every month for our monthly "anniversary" for the entire 1st year. Once we passed the first year marker, he moved it to every year, on the anniversary of when we started dating, but once we had a few wedding anniversaries, the tradition suddenly fizzled. For years we argued, lightheartedly, about how he had gotten apathetic, so when I found the magazine, I had to show him.

Suddenly, it dawned on me that our anniversary had to be coming up soon. It was so uncharacteristic of me to forget our anniversary. Typically, I'm making plans long before the date rolls around, but things were so hectic that we'd lost track of everything, including the date. I looked at John and said, "Oh, my word, I think our anniversary is tomorrow." John, glancing at the calendar on his phone, looked at me in disbelief and said, "Happy Anniversary, it was today." This summed up the chaos of this season of our lives.

When it came time to move into our friends' home, we learned an amazing story of God challenging them to live simply as well. It was a timely testimony with all we were walking through as God established a new normal. Prior to becoming missionaries, Joel was a professional basketball player overseas. They were planning to build their dream house on a piece of land they purchased. They started with a guest suite over the 2-car garage and planned on building their home next to it. After becoming missionaries, they realized they no longer needed a bigger home. The 700-square-foot guest suite above the 2-car garage was sufficient. They converted the dining room to the master bedroom using a shelf to create a partition since there was no wall or door. They put in a trap door at the foot of the bed that led to a vertical ladder going downstairs, where they converted the one side of the 2-car garage into a bedroom for their 4 kids. God found it perfect to choose us to move in to look after it. After living in a 3,000-square-foot house, we could use the simplicity.

During this time, funds were so tight we often wondered if we would have money for weekly groceries. Sometimes we didn't, but during this time, God was so faithful. He would move someone's heart to bring us veggies from their garden or a dinner even though they had no idea we were in need. Our parents would take our kids clothes shopping or buy groceries on their way to visit. Somehow we always got through, and these gifts always came at a critical time.

Though we were devastated in losing our home, we were also seeing clearly for the first time. We had no idea how we had been so blind. Maybe as the "stuff" we accumulated piled up, it blocked our view from seeing those around us in desperate need, and only once it was gone could we see how entangled we were by all of it. Though we lived simply, we didn't realize how much more we could've given after our *basic* needs of food and shelter were met. Maybe we could've forgone a vacation and given it away, or reduced our monthly bills by being content instead of "needing" more, or given our tax return away instead of upgrading our kitchen with granite countertops.

Not that any of these things are wrong in themselves, but the tendency to become more self-focused and less others-focused is hard to recognize, though we started to see it reflected in our lack of *sacrificial* giving.

I know God allowed the loss of our home and our source of income as a way of stripping off the things that were entangling us, hindering us from doing the work of His kingdom. At this point, we had been stripped completely of every entanglement that wasn't rooted in Him. When we literally had no other option but to look up, we saw God show up in amazing ways. Corrie Ten Boom said, "You can never learn that Christ is all you need, until Christ is all you have." How true it is. This was the foundation God was laying in our lives. As hard as it was, we would never change it. We couldn't have learned of His faithfulness in this measure any other way.

CHAPTER 17

FORGET IT FOREVER

"But you must not forget this one thing, dear friends: A day is like a thousand years to the Lord, and a thousand years is like a day. The Lord isn't really being slow about his promise, as some people think. No, he is being patient for your sake. He does not want anyone to be destroyed, but wants everyone to repent." 2 Peter 3:8

"I will never ever pull my promises away from you, never ever says the Lord." ~1st Prophecy

(JOHN): We had finally reached 2009, the season mentioned in the ESPN magazine and the year we hoped the prophetic word would be fulfilled. Would we finally see the breakthrough we had been awaiting all these years? I wrote an email to the head coach and offensive coordinator of every NFL team. Not because I thought they would seriously consider signing me, but if there was a role I was supposed to play, I wanted to be faithful even if I looked crazy. Although I received a few replies kindly telling me no, I'm sure many coaches never opened the email or erased it right after they read it.

The next week I received a call from a number in St Louis. The person in the voice message said, "Hi John, I'm the coach from St. Louis. Please give me a call." Was this the opportunity I had been waiting for? Were the Rams calling me? I returned the call and said, "Hi, this is John Dutton. I'm calling you back."

"Hi, John. I'm a coach with the River City Rage. I got your number from the St. Louis Rams."

"Who is the River City Rage?" I thought to myself. Instead of the email I sent to the Rams hitting the right desk resulting in a call to me for a workout, the Rams sent my number to the coach of the St. Louis indoor league team. To say I was disappointed would be an understatement. The coach said they would love to have me come play for them. This team was in the IFL (Indoor Football League), which was similar to the Arena League but had quite a few differences as well. I got off the phone with the coach and told Terina. After we prayed about it, I took the coach up on his offer and headed out to St Louis. I arrived on Monday, and since the team had gone through a couple of quarterbacks already, I was going to start that Saturday. I had no idea I wouldn't make it past the first game.

In the 2nd quarter, as I went down to grab a ball on the turf, I felt my back tighten up to the point that I could barely move. This had never happened before, and though I did everything I could to loosen it up, nothing worked. I fought through the remainder of the game, but we lost.

The next morning, I awoke to intense pain in my back that was shooting down my left leg. I knew that wasn't a good sign. The following week I tried to practice, but I could barely stand up without unbearable pain.

I was finally able to get an MRI, which revealed that I had a herniated disk in my back. It was the most pain I'd ever experienced. One night, I went out to dinner with some of the players, but the pain was so unbearable I had to find a wheelchair to get around. As I was being wheeled around, I was humiliated, angry, and confused. How did I get to this point? We had sarcastically said all we had left was our health, and now I couldn't even walk.

I talked to the team doctor about my options, which were physical therapy and surgery. Before considering surgery, I consulted with my friend JT Anderson, who operates his own chiropractic office in Denver, Colorado. Since he had a lot of success using this therapy to help with herniated disks, I decided to leave the team and travel to Denver to start treatment.

When I first started the treatment, I had no relief. Up to that point, I had injured my ankles, knee, ribs, and had been hit numerous times in the head. Nothing even remotely compared to this pain. I was uncomfortable every minute of the day. After a few days, Terina and the boys drove out to Colorado. While it was great to see them, it was also difficult to have the kids see me in this condition. I knew it was difficult on them as well.

(TERINA): We were so anxious to see John. Since he was in immense pain, I hated not being there to help. This meant we would be looking for housing, again. Our good friend Jean Wood, who ran a ministry for The Lost Boys of Sudan, let us stay in her vacation condo in the mountains. It couldn't have been a better gift for our family. The kids got to decompress from the stress of the last two years of instability, and John got treatment.

A few months back, we wondered if it was time to look for another agent. I found a Christian sports agent online who happened to be based in Denver. While we were in Denver, we figured John could meet him, of course, since that's what you do when you are contending for an impossible promise regarding playing professional sports and you can hardly walk.

(JOHN): With much hesitation, I decided to talk to the agent. In spite of the fact I hadn't been in the NFL for 10 years, I was 33 years old, and I could barely walk because of the herniated disk, I hobbled up to the office and asked to see the agent, limp and all. Like Abraham, I regarded the fact that my body was as good as dead yet was unwavering in my faith, being fully persuaded God had the power to do what he promised. (Romans 4). Oddly enough, the agent didn't sign me immediately.

(TERINA): When John came back to the car, all we could do was laugh. Crying was certainly a better option, but at this point, we were beyond tears. We genuinely laughed like Sarah did in the Bible when she was told at the age of 90 she would no longer be barren but would give birth to a child. We wondered if God could possibly mean for us to believe the Promise. We knew in the 1st prophecy God stated twice, probably because He knew we would doubt it continually, how He would "never ever pull His promises away from us, never ever." But we felt like Noah, building an enormous ark in the middle of a desert for decades, looking like a fool to everyone around him, yet obeying the word God gave him in spite of it. That was us!

(JOHN): I continued my therapy with little or no relief. I wondered if I would ever be 100% again. One night as we were watching a show on TV, they were praying for healing for people. Terina laid her hand on me and asked God to heal my back. A few days later, I went to my 13th treatment of decompression therapy. It was the same routine, but this time I walked out of the office with no pain whatsoever. It was completely gone. We will never know if it was the prayer, the decompression therapy or both; regardless, I was 100% healed.

We headed back to Northern California and settled in for the fall. I was going into my 3rd year of coaching at COS, but as the football season started, our anticipation continued to grow.

(TERINA): We were certain that any day the call would come. We were finally at the border of our Promised Land, ready to cross over.

During that time, there was talk of the Arena League coming back. Spokane kept calling as they wanted John to be their starting quarterback for the 2010 season.

(JOHN): It had been a year since I had played in the AFL. It was tempting to say yes, but we told the coach what we were waiting for and that I couldn't sign right now. The coach didn't take no for an answer (clearly he lacked the same level of faith I had!) and kept calling me. I told him, "If I am not on an NFL team, I'll sign with Spokane. It would have to be after the Super Bowl."

(TERINA): How we had any faith at all is hard to comprehend, but we had received so many other confirmations we kept choosing to believe. One such confirmation took place at a conference with our ministry partners. After about 40 minutes of prayer and worship together one night, lifting up our situation before the Lord, God spoke the word "crazy" over us to our friend. He said what God was planning to do would be "crazy" and that what God did with Kurt Warner would be small in comparison to what God was going to do with John. As the year progressed, we watched and waited every week, attempting to be unwavering. As you can see from my journal entries below, the wait was hard.

October 23, 2009

"Oh, My Word, we are still waiting. I can't tell you the many things going through my mind right now. On one hand, I'm believing, waiting, hoping, trusting, and, on the other, I wonder if I had it all wrong in the first place. Do I not know your voice? Did I get it all wrong? Is all of this a big coincidence? I don't know! It's almost November, for crying out loud. It's almost halfway over! Come January and it's over. Everything! I would never trust anything I believed was God to be God again: as it says in Timothy "my faith would be shipwrecked." (1 Timothy 1:19) Not my belief in God himself but in recognizing His voice."

November 16, 2009

"I have faith in God that it will happen just as he told me." Acts 27:25

It's been a little while. We weren't expecting to still be waiting, but we are! Yesterday we received an awesome email from our friend Joel. He said he was praying and said he felt God speak to Him that God is *still* writing a story that is going to be one of the greatest stories ever told in sports! He said he saw it happening in front of the largest audience ever on TV, with no one being able to deny it's an absolute miracle. He also said that what God did with Kurt Warner, Rudy, Vince Papale, etc. would somehow pale in comparison to the story. This confirmed an earlier word from Joey.

December 27, 2009

My friend called and said she had a dream that she and her husband were watching John on TV, playing in the NFL. She couldn't remember the team when she woke up! Bummer!

January 18, 2010- Palm Springs

Wow! Can you believe it? We are still waiting. Talk about learning what patience is: trusting in His plan and His timing. The Super Bowl is in three weeks! Without the continual confirmations we have received, we would be 100%, completely without hope. Our son Miki had a dream that Dad was in the NFL. They were showing his AFL highlights and talking about him on ESPN. It was significant because Miki was still learning English at this point. We hadn't owned a TV since he joined our family, so we knew he wouldn't understand the concept of showing highlights from the AFL. Hope renewed once again.

January 22, 2010

Tonight I was wishing I could get a direct reply as to whether it's going to happen this season or not, and I said to John, "I wish I could email Him." John said, "Just pray."

Of course! So last night I prayed that God would specifically speak to me through His word. I opened my Bible directly to Psalm 105 and read the title "God's faithfulness to his people." These are the verses that really ministered to me.

Psalms 105:18-"he forever remembers his covenant, the promise he ordained. *Until the time* the prediction came true the word of the Lord tested him." Vs. 19, Psalms 105:42- "for he remembered his holy promise."

Give me the patience to wait and the faith to believe you will to do as you have spoken.

January 23, 2010-

"Really amazing. Today, it's January 23rd, and you've guessed it... we're still humbly, patiently, and expectantly waiting! We must trust in God and His timing. "His ways are not our ways, and his thoughts are not our thoughts." That's for sure! We will continue to "walk by faith, not by sight. God we trust you. We wait for you. Do not let our hopes be dashed."

January 30th, 2010-

"I am worn out looking for help. My eyes fail looking for my God. May those who hope in you not be disgraced because of me. Oh Lord, the Lord Almighty; may those who seek you not be put to shame because of me for zeal for your house consumes me. Answer me, Lord. Come out of the goodness of your love and, in your great mercy, turn to me. Do not hide your face from your servant; answer me quickly, for I am in trouble." Psalms 69

Four days to the Super bowl...

Still waiting... What more can I say? Aside from it being four days until it's over for this season. I really don't doubt it's going to happen but in 2009? I'm definitely questioning that one! Well, we will know for sure in four days!

"Oh troubled soul, beneath the rod your father speaks, be still be still; learn to be silent unto God, and let him mold you to his will. Oh, praying soul, be still, is still! He cannot break his promised word; sink down into his blessed will and wait patiently on the Lord. Awaiting soul, be still be strong, and though he tarry, trust and wait; doubt not He will not wait too long, fear not, He will not come too late."

When the final whistle blew at Super Bowl XLIV, we were confused and broken. The only reason we were even here was because we stood on the Promise God gave us. We didn't look for it; we didn't ask for it. We simply went to church one night, 10 years prior, not knowing we would be called up onto a stage and prophesied over. So many times along the way, when we *wanted* to let it go or thought we had it wrong and wanted to drop the NFL part and completely forget about it, we'd pray and ask God what to do. He never let us abandon it. He would send confirmations, a word from a friend, a prophecy, a magazine article, a phone call from another player, always something to spur us on to make it hard for us to walk away.

All we wanted was be faithful to Him. And now, we stood here, devastated. At this point we resolved to forget it forever.

CHAPTER 18

BEULAH BEACH

"In any and every circumstance, I have learned the secret of facing plenty and hunger, abundance and need. I can do all things through him who strengthens me." Philippians 4:16

(TERINA): It was over. Everything the last 10 years was building towards was for nothing. We felt like the rug had been yanked out from under us. We had resolved to forget the prophecy forever as it clearly didn't mean what we thought. We no longer talked about it, thought about it, or prayed about it. It was dead, and we felt spiritually and emotionally dead as well. Though it had been well over a year since we lost most of our earthly possessions, the hope of the Promise being fulfilled in 2009 somehow kept us pushing through. Now that we laid the Promise to rest as well, it felt like everything lay in graves. Now what?

(JOHN): Since we had no long-term plan, I figured I could play another season of Arena Football until we figured out what to do. Since we also needed income immediately, this would provide that. A few days after the Super Bowl, I contacted the coach of the AFL Spokane team to inform him I would sign. When I looked over the contract, it didn't match up to the one on which we had originally agreed; there was a discrepancy in salary.

Before the league folded in 2008, I was making around $120,000 per season, about $7,500 per game. Now, only 3 players on each team would receive $1,000 a game; the rest would play for $400 a game. The coach at Spokane, who couldn't wait forever, had given the $1000 to another player and could only offer me the minimum of $400 per game. We weren't sure how we would survive. I respectfully told him no and began looking for another team. At my age, I needed the $1,000 stipend not only because of what I was putting my body through but also because I had a family.

Every team I contacted had already given money to a starting quarterback, except one—the Cleveland Gladiators. I prayed for an open door if Cleveland was where God wanted us. The coach in Cleveland got back to me the next day and offered me a job that included the $1000 stipend per game. Ten years after leaving Cleveland the first time, I was heading back—this time as a Gladiator.

(TERINA): Before signing the contract with Cleveland, we were informed players would lodge in an extended stay hotel and our family would be given the largest available room. Searching the hotel online, we saw the place had up to 3 bedrooms. I decided I could make it if we were given at least one bedroom, so I could have some privacy, which isn't asking too much having 3 boys, though I hoped for the 3-bedroom option. I noticed there was a pool, which I supposed would help cure cabin fever due to having no yard and arriving during Cleveland's winter weather. Everything seemed sufficient for the next 6 months. John signed the contract, and we prepared to leave for Cleveland.

As the departure day drew closer, we noticed the name of the hotel didn't match up with the one we originally looked up. "Hmmm, that's interesting," I thought as I jumped online to probe further. It was then I realized we had, in fact, been looking at the wrong hotel. The hotel the team, including our family, would be staying in had only studios with no private bedroom with a door, no yard, 1 dresser, 1 closet, and no pool for the 3 boys to expend their endless supply of energy. This could not be the next option for our family, particularly after all of the lodging transitions we had previously been through.

I pleaded with John to figure out another option for our family.

(JOHN): I called a friend of mine who lived in Ohio about our situation, hoping he could provide some assistance. He connected us with Beulah Beach, a Camp and Retreat Center that is a part of the Christian Missionary Alliance. Beulah hosts summer camps, retreats, conferences, and special events. Missionaries, both active and retired, also take up residence there. It looked like an incredible place for our family to set up residency with its mission-mindedness and its location, which was only 45 minutes from our practice facility.

The minute Terina saw Beulah online she said, "I know this is it!" It would not only be fun for the kids to live at a camp all season but also encouraging for us as a couple. We desperately needed a community of people who didn't think our work in Africa was abnormal and would, in fact, encourage us to "GO."

While Terina and I both grew up in Christian homes and have amazingly supportive parents, neither of us grew up in a missions-focused environment at home, with our friends, or in our churches, nor can we recall meeting a single missionary until well into adulthood.

As we started our ministry and headed to Africa in 2006, most people didn't understand the calling God had for us. We heard comments about safety, the needs in our own backyard, how this would negatively impact our children and their education, how it wasn't a wise decision, etc. We needed a paradigm shift. Living in a community where overseas ministry was normal became instrumental in us eventually choosing to go.

While talking with the director at Beulah Beach, he said, "I am not sure how we can help you, but drive out. We will figure this out on our knees." We had no idea that God was positioning us at Beulah Beach not simply for a place to live during the football season, but for a much bigger purpose.

(TERINA): About a year after we landed at our friends' home, we were "on the road again" (which has become the theme song our kids play in the car every time we are on a new adventure) with our vehicle loaded down like the Beverly Hillbillies. We ventured east towards Ohio. We made stops along the way at a few places I was sure had never seen a black child with white parents. As they stared at our family as though we were from another planet, I began to wonder if things would be a bit different in the Midwest.

We spent a few long days on the road and finally pulled into the land we would call home off and on for the next 5 years—Beulah Beach Camp and Retreat Center.

(JOHN): We had a great night's sleep in one of the cottages and met up with the director in the morning to receive a tour of the place. We discussed our situation with housing as well as our ministry and concluded us being there was a perfect fit. In exchange for volunteering at Beulah, we were given a 3-bedroom house. Terina helped with the renovations of the cottages, and I cleaned the pool every week. We helped with summer camps and served anywhere there was a need. As we got to know the staff, we recognized God put them in our lives for a reason. Ralph Trainer, the Executive Director, and his family had been missionaries in West Africa for 10 years. Charlotte and Woody Stemple were missionaries in Vietnam. JD and Emily Dueck were missionaries in West Africa, and there were many others. We became friends with so many great people who were living a life sold out for Jesus.

(TERINA): It was incredible to be in an environment where missions were normal, even expected. God said, "Go," so it seemed completely natural to do just that. We had never been surrounded by so many people with a heart for the nations. We watched the sacrifice involved in the Great Commission as missionary families said goodbye to their loved ones, communities, and life in America to *GO* to the ends of the earth, loving and serving the people they lived among. We listened to amazing stories of God working all over the world. We met a retired missionary couple currently living there, who moved to Vietnam a month before the Vietnam War began. They saw American ships pull up to shore and wondered what was happening as this was long before the internet. Though they were encouraged to evacuate, they chose to live for the next ten years in the midst of war. They gave their lives to the people in the community, planted churches, and served at the American bases as well. They had bullet casings land in their yard, and at one point they had to separate, not knowing if they would ever see each other again. We were meeting incredible people, serving in awe-inspiring ways, all over the world.

(JOHN): It was great to be back playing in the Arena League. Because of the pay, a lot of veterans had decided not to come back. This was understandable since the average pay went from around $50,000 to $6,400 and the league was not paying for players' health insurance anymore. Terina and I had prayed about coming back and taking such a huge pay cut, but we felt God was leading us back to the Arena League. The Gladiators had hired Steve Thonn as head coach. Steve had been a coach for a long time in the AFL and was known as a great offensive coach. The Gladiators signed a mix of rookies and veterans including my good friend, Ben Nelson, whom I had played with in Colorado. Even with the low pay and no benefits, once we hit the field, football was football. Physically, I felt good but definitely a little rusty after taking a year off. We finished the season 7-9. While disappointed, I was excited just to be back playing. There were plenty of great moments on the field, but playing also meant that JD's Touchdown Club was back up and running. In 2010, I threw 100 touchdowns and raised over $4,000 for our ministry. As my focus on my career had changed, having a losing record was still very difficult, but knowing that I had made a difference in the lives of others through playing football eased the pain.

(TERINA): I was sewing one afternoon when I heard the words, "Athletes for the Nations." Startled but curious, I thought, "God, are we supposed to partner with them?"

After some research, I realized the ministry didn't exist. God was actually naming our sports' ministry. We wondered if Athletes for the Nations and JD's Touchdown Club would merge somehow. Our ministry work was expanding. We were helping to support children's homes and the street kids' ministry but had never thought about using sports in ministry.

It was during this time we met a couple at Beulah Beach who did sports ministry. We learned of entire teams of players traveling overseas to host camps. Our vision of Athletes for the Nations began to take shape.

Being surrounded by people who had fully given up their lives, comforts, time, and resources for the sake of the Gospel and for others inspired us. It was also a blessing for our children to meet other kids who lived overseas. From their friends, they heard amazing stories of snakes, wild animals, and danger, which gave them the impression our ministry wasn't as abnormal as it seemed in other places we had lived.

It was truly a gift from God. It was also exactly where we needed to be before we would be able to say yes to what God had next.

CHAPTER 19

A SINGLE SPECK OF DUST

"Have I not commanded you? Be strong and courageous. Do not be afraid; do not be discouraged, for the Lord your God will be with you wherever you go." Joshua 1:9

"And I heard the voice of the Lord saying, "Whom shall I send, and who will go for us?" Then I said, "Here I am! Send me." Isaiah 6:8

(TERINA): Two weeks before the final game of John's football season, it became clear we were moving to Ethiopia to further our ministry. While I wished God had revealed it to us earlier in the season so we could have put a little money aside, it would have been difficult to save much when making $16,000 a year. With our 401K drained and our savings account at zero from attempting to survive the Arena Football League suspension, we had no reserves at all. Our last paycheck was only 2 weeks away.

If we went to Ethiopia, John would have to turn down the coaching job at College of the Siskiyou's in the fall, resulting in no paycheck for the next 7 months. How would we survive?

(JOHN): While we had been to Ethiopia for short-term trips, we had never lived there as a family. Though we knew moving our children to a third-world country is never something to take lightly, we were excited. When others heard our plan, they didn't quite share our feelings. We were told it was reckless to move to a third-world country with our kids, and others questioned us on everything from health, safety, our children's education, to why we would take our mission work to Africa when people in the states had needs. At Beulah Beach, however, it was just a way of life.

One morning, while cleaning the pool, I prayed that I would make the right decision. As a father it would impact not only my life but also our family's. As I was praying, I heard very clearly the words "Joshua 1:9 and Isaiah 6:8."

I knew that Joshua 1:9 had something to do with being courageous, but I didn't know anything about the verse in Isaiah. After cleaning the pool, I went directly home to look up the verses. I read in Joshua, "Have I not commanded you? Be strong and courageous. Do not be afraid; do not be discouraged, for the Lord your God will be with you wherever you go." Then I turned to Isaiah 6:8; "Then I heard the voice of the Lord saying, 'Whom shall I send? And who will go for us?' And I said, 'Here am I. Send me!'"

Wow! I had heard from the Lord that I needed to be willing to go and not be afraid. I knew then our family was heading to Ethiopia.

(TERINA): I'll never forget the day John was on the phone, telling the head coach at College of the Siskiyous that since we were going to Africa in the fall, he wouldn't be coaching. As I listened to him talking, my heart started racing as I thought to myself, "We're really doing this! Oh God, I can't believe You're asking us to do this! How will we raise support? We don't even have a sending church?" It's easy to think and talk about doing something that puts my family in a very risky situation; it's difficult, however, to take the step of faith to do it. Right in the middle of that thought and while John was still on the phone, a friend who worked at the camp walked up to me and said, "Hey, I was wondering, how do you and John raise support?" I said, "Funny you ask. As of right now, John is on the phone, turning down his coaching job this fall. After two weeks, we have no source of income. We need to figure out how to raise support *immediately*." He said, "I can set up a speaking event at our church retreat since my dad is the pastor." I couldn't believe the timing. God sent our first speaking engagement and fundraising opportunity the very moment John was turning down his job. It was His way of saying, "I've got this!" We ended up speaking at their retreat and received our first donations towards the trip.

The only time we could go to Ethiopia for an extended period of time was during John's offseason, so we needed to leave as soon as possible to accomplish everything before the start of the next season. We needed funding quickly. Finding a great price on tickets, we felt God asking us to sell our only vehicle to purchase them.

Considering we were in the middle of adopting Solomon, and when we returned we would need a car for our family, this seemed both foolish and risky. We would never have enough money to buy a car when we got back, particularly one large enough to fit four children. We would be completely dependent on God putting it on someone's heart to *give* us a car or donate enough money for us to buy one! As we weighed this decision, I pictured trying to take public transportation to get kids to school, practices, games, etc. while John took the bus to practice, a 45 minute drive a way. We could not make it without a car!

Ultimately, we obeyed and put our car up for sale. I prayed it wouldn't sell...unless this was *the only option*. It sold within the week. Now we faced another large obstacle —lodging. We had zero funds and no short-term rental options. In Ethiopia, an entire year's rent is required up front. We only needed 4 months, not 12. Unless we found a short-term rental, which was very rare, we would either have to pay an additional $7000 for 8 months we wouldn't even use or rent out a hotel, which would be equally as expensive. Both weren't options. We needed a short-term rental, but how would we find it? Craigslist or Zillow were not available. Once again, we needed God to make a way. Our missionary partners, Joey and Destiny LeTourneau, who were living in Ethiopia, helped us look for a place. With less than 2 weeks until our departure date, they hadn't found anything. Everyone was asking us, "What are you going to do? Are you going to cancel? What if you don't find anything? Are you flipping out?"

Ultimately, we decided we were going with or without set plans. We knew He would direct our steps. The Lord had been training us to trust Him this way for years. It wasn't uncommon for us to load up the car with our bags and drive not knowing where we were going to stay, having no money for more than a few days in a hotel. The first time God asked us to "go" without having a place to live was the first year we moved out to California for four months so John could coach at the College of the Siskiyous. We loaded up our bags and drove West. When we arrived, we decided to camp for a few days while we waited to see what He would provide. While we tried not to question how He would provide a furnished place for only 4 months, we just knew He would.

God ended up opening up a door for a house that was for sale. It was staged so it already had furniture; all we had to do is move in. This was the first time we took a wild leap of faith, and God demonstrated His faithfulness.

God also strategically placed us down the street from Jeff and Jen Summers, a family that would eventually become some of our best friends. When we first arrived, we read an article in the paper about a family who had just moved to town with 3 children they had just adopted from Africa. As we read the article, we said, "We have to meet them!" Since Miki had just joined our family a month before, we worried he would be the only African-American child in the area and that we would be the only mixed family. Not long after we moved in, our kids were out on the street playing, when they came running in, yelling, "Mom, you know that family we saw in the paper? They live on our street!" Sure enough, their kids also ran home to tell their parents a family down the street looked just like their family! Of all the places He could've placed us, it happened to be on the exact street as this other family. Every year we moved out West, we did the same thing: We loaded up our car and drove out, bringing no furniture, just a bag for each of us and some basic necessities. We recalled His faithfulness in the past and waited to see Him open a door again. We just hoped it would be before we left for Ethiopia.

(JOHN): One morning before leaving for Africa, we got an email from the LeTourneau's. They had met a missionary couple who happened to be leaving on a three-month furlough the *exact* day we planned on arriving, and they needed someone to stay in their place. What are the chances?! While we weren't sure what that meant for the last month, we were excited to have a place solidified for now. Even more incredible was how, in a capital of over 7 million people, the Lord provided housing only a few doors down from the LeTourneau's. Once God provided the place, we no longer worried about how we would pay for it. Since He clearly wanted us in Ethiopia, He would provide.

Prior to leaving, a friend of ours was leading a men's Bible study on the book *Radical* by David Platt. The book challenges its readers to raise funds by going through their houses and donating excesses. After this Bible study group took the challenge, they sent us a check from the proceeds. The check was the exact amount we needed for our housing with a little change left over!

(TERINA): We drove out to Illinois to speak at a church and we stayed with a wonderful family there. On the way, as we drove past the Creation Museum, I thought how awesome it would be to take the kids, though I knew it wasn't the right time with trying to raise funds to go to Ethiopia. During our stay, the family asked us if we had ever been to the Creation Museum, as they knew we drove by it on our way to their house. I told them we hadn't, and they encouraged us to go. I simply smiled and said, "That would be fun," thinking, "Not this time, though!"

The next morning, after speaking at the church, we packed up our vehicle to leave. As we said our goodbyes and drove away, we noticed a card lying in our cup holder. We opened it up and found a $100 bill to "enjoy the museum." I was shocked! What a thoughtful gift.

However, as we were driving, we weighed what to do. We wanted to honor the gift and enjoy the Creation Museum, but we barely had money for dinner, hotel, and gas. Spending money on an activity like the Creation Museum was problematic. We talked it through and decided we needed to honor the gift.

When we arrived at the museum, I sheepishly asked the woman at the front desk if any discounts were available for those in full time ministry as we were desperate for any savings at all. Sometimes faith-based businesses have a pastor's rate or missionary rate. She told us they didn't but asked me to wait a second. Reaching for something under the counter, she pulled out a sealed white envelope and, enthusiastically, placed it in our hands. She said, "I'm so thrilled to meet you. We have been waiting for you for over 2 weeks." "What?" I thought, somewhat confused. She continued, "Two weeks ago, an individual who wanted to gift a family with tickets to the museum told us to pray for God to show us that family. It's been over 2 weeks, and I have been curious about whom God had chosen to use the tickets. Then she said, "You're that family!" I was amazed as I imagined God orchestrating this visit over 2 weeks ago. We ended up going to the Creation Museum and having money to get home.

As I lay in the planetarium learning about all the planets, galaxies, Milky Way and seeing our entire solar system reduced to smaller than a single point in scale to our universe, I was reminded how we were not even the size of a single speck of dust in comparison. I was overcome with emotion, completely unable to fathom how the God of the entire universe would take the time to orchestrate events in our lives this way. Why did He even care? I felt so small, yet so incredibly valuable to Him in that moment, seeing how He sent His Son not only to die for me but also to lavish love on our family in such a special way. It was a moment we would need to remember in the midst of the trials to come. Even though we are smaller than a single speck of dust, He *is* with us, and He *will* provide.

CHAPTER 20

HE CHOSE THE FOOLISH

"For consider your calling, brothers: not many of you were wise according to worldly standards, not many were powerful, not many were of noble birth. But God chose what is foolish in the world to shame the wise; God chose what is weak in the world to shame the strong; God chose what is low and despised in the world, even things that are not, to bring to nothing things that are, so that no human being might boast in the presence of God." 1 Corinthians 1:26-29

"Immediately they left their nets and followed Him." Matthew 4:20 NASB

(TERINA): After a long journey across the ocean, we landed in Ethiopia, kids in tow, after traveling for nearly two days. Though we were half a world away, somehow it felt even farther than that from home. We were relieved to get all 15 pieces of luggage through the often-shady bag "security" and load up the van to head to our new home. Anytime you drive at night feels strange, particularly in a place so foreign. I watched as my kids stared out the window, wondering what was going through their heads. Since it was their first taste of poverty, a weighty silence permeated the car. When we finally arrived at our new Ethiopian home, we unloaded our belongings and settled into bed for the night.

(TERINA): Waking up the first morning in Ethiopia was surreal. I couldn't believe we were actually living in Africa! The sound of a rooster crowing, announcing the new day, was the first thing I noticed. It was hard not to. Clearly, this rooster took its job seriously, making sure anyone within a 500-yard radius could hear it at the earliest crack of dawn. That rooster was going to become dinner if it did this for the next 4 months straight!

I dragged myself out of bed to open the patio door as I was curious to see the surroundings outside. The warm air, mixed with a trace of fresh smoke, came pouring into the room and filled my senses with a feeling of anticipation. It was a new adventure for our family. I took in all the unfamiliar sights and sounds: the scraping sound of a small make shift broom (consisting of a bundle of sticks tied together) as the cleaner swept the patio, the clip-clop sound of a horse pulling a cart as the driver snapped the whip, and the unharmonious tune from the *Bajaj's*, a small three-wheeled cabin cycle that crams up to 6 people inside as they weave in and out of traffic. You could hear various animal noises of donkeys, sheep, and goats as they strolled along the streets, their shepherds following close behind. It was a whole different world, and I couldn't wait to share it with my children.

(JOHN): It took us a few weeks to settle in as a family, but our ministry work started immediately. We began strengthening our on-the-ground relationships with the ministries with whom we were partnered.

We spent time at the children's home to love on the kids, worship with them, and communicate current needs to those back in the states. We served alongside the LeTourneaus in their ministry with the street kids, assisting with the opening of the boys' shelter and in the launching of a church plant. Because most of the street kids were ashamed of their tattered clothes, shoeless feet, and dirty faces, they wouldn't dare step foot into a church. Therefore, Joey and Destiny opened a church service where all street kids could come and feel loved and be a part of His family. This time of fellowship, worship, and loving on them gave me a bigger picture of God's heart for the broken, the lost, the least of these, and learning to be physically His hands and feet to them was an honor.

(JOHN): One way God was teaching us to hear His voice and obey was joining in on "walking the streets with Isaiah 58," an idea Joey and Destiny had to allow the Holy Spirit to show us who to minister to as we walked the streets, based on Isaiah 58. It wasn't a primary part of our ministry, as we all were devoted to the long-term commitment of empowering and transforming the lives of the children we served, but, whenever we asked God to whom He wanted to minister, He would direct us to them. One day our son Miki headed out with our guard, Kebede, this time to bring food (Isaiah 58:7).

While it isn't possible to meet the needs of every hungry person on our own, we could do what God was asking of us. It was getting dark, and Miki and Kebede had been gone for hours. They were getting ready to give up for the night when the Lord urged Kebede to visit a lady in his church. Upon arriving at her home, they were shocked. Her kids were crying in hunger, and she had been praying for God to send help that night. Because Miki and Kebede were listening, God led them to this lady. They were His hands and feet in physically meeting her desperate cry for help. Week after week, stories such as this would emerge as we realized answering people's prayers was what God desired to do through us! I questioned how many people didn't receive God's answer, not because it wasn't His will, but because we weren't actively listening and *responding* in action.

(TERINA): During this time, God challenged us to move forward in ways that were outside of our wisdom, skill set, and training. While we read in the Bible how God often chooses the fools, the unlearned, and unqualified to do His work, not as common to see this approach used in ministry today. Instead, we design strategies and plans that can be accomplished based on our own qualifications, plans, and implementation, leaving little room for failure, or dare I say, God to make up the difference. By doing so, we unavoidably remove accomplishing anything dependent on God's power and action.

God was getting ready to school us in His way of ministry. A few years prior, a pastor prophesied over John and said, "God is telling you He is requiring two things from you: 'Hear His voice and obey.'" We were being taught to conduct our lives and ministry in a way that demonstrated our trust in His leading, even when we weren't qualified or even when it seemed foolish to the world. This way brought Him glory, *not* our wisdom, training, and qualifications.

Moving to Ethiopia, without funds, housing, airline tickets, salaries, or a set plan was only the beginning. It was like the disciples when Jesus stood on the shore and said, "Come, follow Me." They didn't have time to raise funds or plan out how they would follow him; they hadn't developed a fail proof ministry strategy, nor didn't get their families' approval. They simply heard His voice and obeyed, *immediately* dropping their nets and following Him. How much were we willing to trust Him and His power?

(JOHN): Before our trip to Ethiopia, we had a vision of opening a guesthouse *one day,* as in *years* down the road. Nevertheless, after much prayer, we got the impression we would be opening one on *this* trip.

We had no degree in hotel management, business, or marketing, and opening a guesthouse in a third-world country halfway around the world, without the funds and with only a few months to work, was a recipe for disaster—but God. The first step was to look at properties. We found one we liked and had a meeting to sign a contract.

The day before, Terina prayed, "Lord, if there is another building you have for us, please make it known before we move forward." Before she finished praying, Kebede, our guard, informed her, in broken English, of a property he wanted us to see. As we stepped into the gate, we knew it was the place.

We were in need of funds for two of our projects: rent for the home we were in the process of opening for the street boys and a year's rent for the guesthouse. Sure enough, someone donated funds to cover rent for the boys' home, which enabled us to move forward on the guesthouse. Soon after, we moved in and began hiring staff.

(TERINA): After hiring staff, we prayed for God to give us the wisdom to train them. We had never run a guesthouse, let alone trained others to do it. We needed Him to show us the next step.

It was during this time that I received a phone call from a very successful guesthouse that had grown to four locations, looking for overflow housing for some incoming guests. The manager wanted to rent our facilities and bring in their staff to run all of the operations. We quickly realized God had sent our training directly to us. We told our staff, "Watch everything they do!" The manager allowed our employees to help their staff, which gave them hands-on experience. We paid attention to every detail of how they ran all operations and guest services. By the time their staff and guests departed, the framework of our operations and guest services were in place. We couldn't have orchestrated a better training!

The next step was bringing in guests to fill the place. We asked God to show us what to do and prayed, "Lord this is yours. Whether you bring one guest or five hundred, it's in your hands!" About a week later, a travel agent from the states, who completed bookings for adoptive families and short-term mission trips, called and said, "I don't know if you are interested, but I could have your guesthouse completely booked in March." Of course, I said yes! From March on, we were full for the entire first year!

The final piece was hiring our manager, which happened after we returned to the states. I tried not to question God's timing in not raising up someone prior to us leaving, but how would I find an employee from half way around the world?

The travel agent helping us book guests was traveling to Ethiopia and knew about our urgent need for a Guesthouse Manager. While there, she had coffee with a former employee of an adoption agency she was working with on her adoption. During the conversation, she discovered he had quit his job, that very day, due to the corruption. When she asked him what he planned to do, he said, "I don't know, but God will provide." After inquiring about his degree, he told her it was in hotel management and tourism! He had no idea of her connection to us or the brand-new guesthouse, so she was shocked! She abruptly excused herself to call me about whether or not to set up an interview with our ministry partners. I told her, "Yes!" He ended up being our manager.

(JOHN): Terina and I had both met Solomon, now our son, on two previous trips to Ethiopia. Prior to leaving for this upcoming trip to Ethiopia, it dawned on us, if we completed our home study before we left for Ethiopia, he could move in with our family during our time there and return to the United States with us. We needed to make this happen! The only problem was we didn't have $3,000 for a home study, in addition to the funds for shots, background checks, etc. Even more, the time a home study typically takes to complete would far surpass the time remaining before we left. We had no funds and no time. We prayed and felt God leading us to move forward, in spite of how it appeared. We worked on our home study, met with a social worker, collected paperwork, did background checks, ran fingerprints, filled out stacks of forms, and got every piece notarized in record time.

(TERINA): Our social worker knew about our timeline and was deeply concerned about a form we needed, one that usually took around 40 days to receive back from our state, which was pony express slow. We needed it sooner than that in order to complete the adoption before we left for Ethiopia. Then Solomon could move in with us while we were there and also return to the states with us. We fasted and prayed. The form came back 3 days later!

(JOHN): When we went to do fingerprints, we had less than $500 in our account. Shots were $200 each, leaving us with less than $100 to our name. Since we knew this adoption was a part of God's plan, we wrote the check and prayed for His continued provision. When we handed the check to our social worker, he told us the fee was on him and gave it back! He not only covered the fee for our fingerprints, but also he waived the $3,000 home study fee as well! We finished all the adoption requirements prior to leaving for Ethiopia. Finally, after our family had lived in the country for two months, Solomon was coming home!

(TERINA): It had been 2 years since I first spotted Solomon in a home of 162 boys, far out in the bush of Ethiopia. I knew instantly he was my child. Now, the car carrying him pulled up to the gate to bring him to us. When Solomon stepped out of the car, Zach and Drew burst out the door, practically tackling him to give him the biggest hug. We couldn't believe after two long years he was joining our family.

(TERINA): A few weeks prior to heading back to the states, we received a notice that stated if we didn't have the remaining $7,200 balance paid for Solomon's adoption in 48 hours, our case wouldn't go to embassy before we left, meaning Solomon would have to stay behind for now, regardless of the fact he had lived with us for 2 months. We, of course, did not have anywhere near that amount, so we sent out a newsletter and prayed. The very next day we received an email that we were receiving a grant for $3,500 from Lifesong for Orphans. Other family and friends gave towards the adoption as well. We paid the balance with some change left to spare. We actually laughed out loud (like Sarah in the Bible) when we got the invoice that said "PAID IN FULL!" ONLY GOD!

(JOHN): With only a few weeks left before we were heading home, we still needed a car and had no funds to purchase one. During our time in Ethiopia, a couple came to visit us and asked about our car situation. This generous couple ended up giving us the funds to purchase a car when we arrived home.

Now, one last obstacle remained—the U.S. Embassy appointment. At this time, appointments were only scheduled on Thursdays, which left only two Thursdays available before our departing flights. You don't just call and schedule an appointment; you wait for them to set a date. It could take weeks, months, sometimes even a year or longer.

Sure enough, we got the last possible Embassy appointment, four days before we were heading back to America.

The day of our Embassy appointment, there was a "high alert" in the city due to a terrorist attack threat, particularly targeting foreigners. We were told to avoid all areas Westerners would be, including the U.S. Embassy. We prayed about what to do, as it felt dangerous to drive directly to where there was a threat. God said to go, and we obeyed. I'll never forget driving up the street towards the U.S. Embassy, seeing that American flag waving in the wind. The feeling was of unimaginable gratitude for being born in such a wonderful country. While no country is perfect, and the people within can still choose to do evil no matter where they live, the principles of equality, freedom, and justice for all are still the principles our flag represents and are often taken for granted until living in places where these principles are lacking. That day, the flag symbolized security and safety. In the midst of a terrorist attack threat, we felt protected. After a long wait at the Embassy, we passed. Our growing family was going home!

(TERINA): We had seen God do so much in a short time, all things we would've missed out on had we not been willing to obey His leading.

It wasn't wise, safe, or comfortable to move forward in the ways He had asked, but as we learned to hear His voice and obey, we saw His power, not our own, as He chose the foolish and unqualified to bring Him glory.

CHAPTER 21

A KERNEL OF WHEAT

*"Let us hold unswervingly to the hope we profess,
for He who promised is faithful"* Hebrews 10:23

*"Very truly I tell you, unless a kernel of wheat falls to the ground
and dies, it remains only a single seed.
But if it dies, it produces many seeds."* John 12:24

(JOHN): Going to church in Africa is not for the faint of heart. Typically, services last for at least 3 to 4 hours, if not more, depending on the schedule of speakers. Since the service is spoken in Amharic, the Ethiopian national language, it's difficult to comprehend anything being said. Therefore, we spend our time worshipping with the congregation for the first few hours and then read our Bibles while they preach for a few hours more. The children are also expected to sit there for the entire service, so our kids brought their Bibles, a pen, and a journal to give them something to do, which they did amazingly! While attending a service one evening, approximately 2 1/2 hours into it, I suddenly heard English, which immediately caught my attention. I had no idea it would be specifically directed towards me until the pastor said, "Brother John, the Lord just gave me a word for you."

My heart began beating rapidly. He said, "All that I have told you that I am going to do, I'm going to do! Everything I said that is going to happen, is going to happen! I am faithful. Miracles will take place! There was a time where you were in the wilderness. I used that to train you for the ministry I have prepared for you. I am a faithful God. I want your total trust because I am faithful! I will do all that I have promised. I am going to bless you abundantly. You are going to see my goodness. I will give you many good things. I am a good God. And as a confirmation of my word, I will fill you with joy."

(TERINA): As He spoke these words to John, we both cried, along with our son Zach, who was old enough to understand the significance of the prophecy. Because the Promise was dead to us since the Super Bowl the year before, we hadn't allowed ourselves to go *there*. That night, however, in the middle of an Ethiopian church service, the Lord spoke again. After the service, Pastor Yonas came up to John and me and said, "I just want to confirm that God is telling you He *is* faithful, and He *is* going to fulfill everything He has spoken. You can *fully* trust Him."

Our hope in the original Promise was resurrected.

(JOHN): Having just moved back from Ethiopia, where a combination of an Ethiopian diet, training at a 7,000 ft. elevation, and walking everywhere, resulted in me being in the best shape of my adult life, I couldn't wait for the season to start.

Our first game was in Spokane, Washington, facing the Shock. The game was off to a great start, and I felt the best I had felt in a long time. Three quarters into the game, I had already thrown 6 touchdowns. I thought to myself, "Maybe my rebound is finally coming!" We had possession of the ball, and I was going for our 7th touchdown when I felt *it*. Right after I released the ball, it felt like someone had just kicked me in the left calf, and I immediately fell to the ground.

I thought to myself, "This is going to be a bad charley horse." My intention was to walk it off, but when I stood up to walk to the bench, it felt like my heel sunk a foot into the ground. I waived a teammate over to help me off the field.

(TERINA): Watching the game at a friend's house since it was out of town, I was delighted in the way things were going. After receiving another word from the pastor in Ethiopia and seeing the shape John was in, I felt as excited as I had ever been. This was it for sure! The team was playing great, and John looked spectacular. As I watched the TV screen, I suddenly noticed the back-up quarterback was in. "What happened?" I asked, bewildered. The broadcasters projected the coaches were giving him a rest. I, however, knew this wasn't usual. The starting QB does not get pulled out during the middle of a game when he's playing great and they haven't sealed the win. *What is happening right now?!*

(JOHN): Immediately recalling stories I'd heard about people tearing their Achilles, I knew it was exactly what just happened. I hadn't even made it through a single game. My season was over. I called Terina and broke down in tears.

(TERINA): I couldn't believe my ears. I knew my friend couldn't possibly understand all we had been through for the last 13 years leading up to this injury, so I had to get out of there, fast. It wasn't just an injury; it was *so much more*. The only thing I could think of at this moment was the bonfire I was about to light in my front yard with every journal I had ever written about this Promise. What fools! I gathered my kids, said my goodbyes as calmly as possible, and stormed home.

Once again we were back at Ground Zero. How would he ever recover from an Achilles injury at this age?

Journal Entry from this time...

"Is it ever going to happen? I want to shred or burn my journals! It feels like one big joke on us, seriously! What the heck! I have nothing to say, seriously, nothing! How can we be 'blessed in the sports world' when John continues to lead the league in interceptions every year? How about not having a winning season in the last five seasons? Oh wait, we won the division last year, but, oh, I forgot, John tore his Achilles in the first game of the season so the rookie backup helped lead them to a division title, of course! I find it particularly interesting that John actually felt good for the first season in years. His weight was down, and he was in great shape so of course it would go just that way! Poor guy. He's tried so hard and has hung in there for so long. For what? I'm really trying to believe in the Promise, but it's SOOOOO hard, game after game, season after season, and year after year to continue to spur him on, reminding him of what God has said, encouraging him not to give up. 'Maybe this is the year,' I'd say, only to have it not be, year after year after year."

"Hope deferred makes the heart sick. **WELL I'M SICK!!!** I'm tired of believing and being there to remind him, time after time, like a broken record, only to continue to see nothing happen. I'M DONE! What do I have to say? What can I say that I haven't said 1 million times before? I've hung on for years, believing, trusting, against ALL hope, and still there's no breakthrough. I've knocked on the doors of heaven, I've prayed, I've stood firm on the Promise, I've helped John up over and over and over and over and over. Are my words even meaningful at this point? I have nothing to say! Good night!" I clearly wasn't in the finest place I'd ever been!

(JOHN): Not only did we think the Promise was over, but also that my AFL career was in jeopardy. Even more, I stewed over how active I would be after recovering from this injury. The turn of events left me speechless. Over the next couple of days, I met with doctors, set up my surgery, and discussed my options for rehab, which they said would be a minimum of 8 long months.

(TERINA): It was during this season that I was up in the stands asking God for a very clear Gideon's fleece that night at the game. We just couldn't take any more. This Promise felt like it was going to put an end to us. I needed something so concrete, a fleece so certain that I could never question again what God meant by the 1st prophecy. As I sat in the stands, I asked God to send me a sign that night regarding John in the NFL specifically. It was then, God sent His angel to hand deliver our plaque that said, "Keep the Faith."

Now we could do nothing but hold out in hope that "He who promised is faithful!"

(TERINA): With the injury, JD's Touchdown Club was finished for the season. "Well, there goes our only fundraiser of the year," I concluded as though God hadn't thought it through. Why, in times of trial, loss, and setbacks do we forget the bigger picture? What I should've immediately remembered was that God uses *every single* failure, disappointment, setback, and loss for our good, for our growth, and always for the benefit of others. He never stops "working things together for *good*," in the midst of our trials. He wastes nothing.

Once I got my head together, I prayed, "Okay, God, I know there's a bigger purpose in this. What is our role?" Sure enough, He showed us. As always, His idea was brilliant compared to ours.

At the time, JD's Touchdown Club was about John being significant by using his touchdowns to raise money for the ministry. After the injury, we realized we could ask John's teammates to allow their success on the field to raise funds.

Ooohhhh! I had that moment of revelation when your unknowingly narrow vision is expanded. Why would we be satisfied with only John being an Athlete for the Nations when we could get his teammates involved as well? Don't we want them to use their success to be significant?

(JOHN): So I presented the idea to the guys on my team and had a few guys sign up and start receiving pledges. Russel Monk, our fullback, was one of the players that had signed up for AFTN and was raising funds for every rushing touchdown he made. I was on the bench with my crutches watching one of our games, and Russ scored a touchdown. While everyone was cheering and celebrating, Russ walked back to the bench and came up to me and said, "JD, do you know what I was thinking after that touchdown?" I was used to guys celebrating and making a show, so I wasn't sure where he was going with it until he said, "I just thought of how much money I raised for other people!" That is exactly what AFTN is about: Getting athletes of all ages, all sports, and all skill levels to get their eyes off their own success and to fix their eyes on helping others. Here we were, in the middle of a professional football game, and Russ was not only being successful but also being significant. God continued to expand our vision of AFTN by showing us we could get athletes on every team, in every sport, at every level to be an Athlete for the Nations! Now *that* is making a difference! Though the injury set me back on the field, it took Athletes for the Nations much further than I ever imagined, and it gave me strength as I endured the long process of rehabilitation.

(TERINA): Watching John endure the pain of recovery was hard. He didn't sleep at night, and, when he did, he groaned as the nerves in his legs fired continually. He would get angry, hit his fist against the wall or wake up in a full-on sweat. It was difficult to see him that way.

(JOHN): Rehab on this injury was tough. From first trying to pick up marbles with my toes, to the agonizing deep massages to break up the scar tissue, to the intense workouts to gain my strength back, I was physically and mentally exhausted. I'd lie awake at night in pain, while the nerves fired down my legs, attempting to rewire. It felt as though I hadn't slept thoroughly in months. They pushed me hard! Because I was recovering so quickly, the coach and trainer talked of me coming back by playoffs.

Through much prayer, discussion with my coach and trainers, and debate with Terina and my family, I ended up suiting up for the first playoff game. At the end of the 3rd quarter, the quarterback was benched as we were down by 21 points, and I ended up getting called back into the game, only four months after my injury. I threw 3 touchdowns in the 4th quarter, and we came within one score of winning the game. To play in a game only 4 months after surgery for an Achilles tear is unheard of. Apparently, God wanted to secure the fact I wasn't done playing. The season ended with an invitation to play for the Gladiators another season.

(TERINA): God used John's injury, his "falling to the ground," to expand our vision that every athlete, at every level, could use their success on the field to be significant off of it. John had become a single kernel of wheat that, literally, fell to the ground that day. His season died, his fundraiser died, his hope nearly died, but through it, many other Athletes for the Nations were produced. It became our vision not only for John but also for every athlete, at every level, in every sport around the world to turn their success to significance.

Athletes for the Nations was born!

CHAPTER 22

YET LOWER STILL

There was a time where you were in the wilderness. I used that to train you for the ministry I have prepared for you. ~Prophecy in Ethiopia

"But remember the former days, when, after being enlightened, you endured a great conflict of sufferings, sometimes you were publicly exposed to ridicule and persecution; at other times you were partners with those who were so treated...So do not throw away this confident trust in the Lord. Remember the great reward it brings you! For you have need of endurance, so that when you have done the will of God you may receive what is promised."

(TERINA): *"Yet lower still"* were the words I heard as I was praying one morning in regards to what God had next. Since John and I had spent what felt like an entire lifetime in the wilderness, hearing these words made my heart sink. *"Yet lower still,"* I repeated in exasperation.

"How much lower are we going?" I recalled studying the process of laying a foundation after we received the first prophecy, which I discov-

ered would require crushing, breaking, and ripping out the old one before the ground could be prepared for the new foundation He was going to lay. So *this* was what we had to look forward to? *Great!*

(JOHN): While we had already been stripped of our personal possessions, I still was a professional athlete, and I, unknowingly, found a piece of my identity in that place. This humbling process of going lower meant that any part of my identity not rooted in Him would need to be ripped out as well, including every piece built around the approval of others.

The 2012 AFL season was quite possibly the worst season to date. At the start of the season, a labor dispute erupted between the league and its players in regards to salaries and benefits. The very first televised game, both teams' players refused to play. This caused the owners and coaches to find replacement players at the last moment, including some coaches. To say the least, it was a complete embarrassment to the entire league. It was particularly disheartening to see the Arena League in such disarray, especially since so many players, past and present, worked hard to build the league.

Later in the season, my team got caught right in the middle of the dispute. A few hours before we were to report for a home game, a majority of our team voted to forfeit the game, unannounced, and didn't show up to play. Terina and I prayed about what God would want me to do. We both felt Him telling us that a more honorable way existed to solve the issue. I felt the way the team was doing it was not only a disgrace to the league and our team but also a dishonor to our fans.

From that game on, a division existed amongst our team, which was primarily directed at me. My goal was to handle the labor dispute the right way and question if there were other ways to be heard without acting dishonorably. Clearly, I wanted better pay for the players, but I cared more about the future of the league. I had spent 12 years attempting to build the reputation of the league, but many of these younger players could care less about how it would affect the league as a whole. I attempted to mediate between the owners, players, and coaches to see what options were possible aside from a boycott.

The weeks after the strike, I struggled coming to work every day due to the division between me and quite a few other players. My performance on the field reflected this battle. Eventually, I was benched for a game, which led players to tell me I was getting what I deserved. It bothered me tremendously, because in 31 years of playing football, I always put my team first and treated my teammates with respect and loyalty. To have teammates turn their backs on me was difficult, affecting me both on and off the field.

(TERINA): Watching John get benched was the final nail in the coffin for me. I couldn't take any more! The coaches and owners told the players if they didn't show up for the game, it would hurt the franchise as well as the league as a whole. John attempted to mediate between all the parties involved to work out a mutually beneficial solution. It felt like a slap in the face when the backup quarterback, who led the strike, was named the starter near the end of the season after John was benched. We know the sport of football owes no one anything, but for it to go down that way shocked me.

I personally thought sending some of the players to Africa to see how people all over the world live would put their "injustice" in perspective. We were stuck in the middle of dealing with issues of real job injustice—seeing crippled children forced to beg in the streets by their pimp who manipulated their handicap for profit, or meeting 12-year-old girls who were forcibly sold for sex every night to put food on the table of their families, or learning of entire families whose lives consist of holding a job as forced slaves in brickyards and factories where they will never escape. Most of the world lives on less than $2 a day, and over 1 billion people attempt to live on less than $1 a day. Making $10,066 a year means you live in the top 16% in the world in wealth. Even the poorest Americans are rich. It made hearing the players' plight of "inequity" a challenge regarding how to respond.

(JOHN): My final game as a Gladiator ended with me getting benched in the 2nd quarter and watching the guy who led the strike finish the game by tossing the ball off the net for a last-second touchdown for the win. It was a surreal ending to all that had happened that year. Eventually, the strike resulted in players receiving a little more pay, but in the five years that would follow since the strike, the league dwindled from 17 teams to 5.

(JOHN): Though I knew my time in Cleveland was over, God used this experience to root my identity in Him, not in the approval of others. I experienced, for the first time, the opposition that comes from choosing to stand on my convictions. It was here He developed the courage in me to choose to suffer opposition, slander, being misunderstood, and the accusations that come by going against the majority.

We all have decisions to make, and it takes courage to do what we feel is right, particularly when in the minority. From a teenager standing his ground as his peers pressure him to do something he knows he shouldn't, to a politician making the right, moral decision for the masses and not simply for his or her own political position, to a person choosing to speak up about what they believe is right knowing they may be slandered, accused, misunderstood, and even hated—doing the right thing is hard. Far too many people compromise their beliefs when making decisions for personal gain or the approval of others. This was a very tough time as I sought God and did what He would want me to do. It was not popular with my teammates, but through the slander and the division, God was teaching me to always stand up for what I believe is right in the eyes of God, not only for myself but also for everyone involved. I learned that losing identity in the world and finding it in Christ alone is almost always a painful process. Though He brought me lower, it was only through this that He could raise me up to where He needed me to be.

CHAPTER 23

WHAT IS IT

"He humbled you, causing you to hunger and then feeding you with manna" Deuteronomy 8:3

"Take nothing for your journey, no staff, nor bag, nor bread, nor money; and do not have two tunics." Luke 9:3

(TERINA): Our time in Cleveland was over. We prayed about whether or not to move to the West Coast, closer to our families, or head to Denver, where many of our ministry partners had relocated over the past few months. We were just beginning to serve in full-time ministry and decided being around others we worked with was a great choice.

(JOHN): Like every year before, we hoped this would be the year the Promise was fulfilled, and I faithfully put my body through rigorous training. We had received the Keep the Faith plaque a year before, and to add to our anticipation of something happening, Terina's mom, during a 3 day fast, had a vision, something she'd never had before. In it, she saw two different scenes, appearing like an old-fashioned slide show. The first scene was what appeared to be a helmet and a large white horse. She thought it was possibly the Denver Broncos helmet but wasn't sure. In the second scene, she saw a paper with a large hand sweeping across the page down to the bottom where there was an X. She recognized it was an NFL contract, and I was signing it. We had no idea what this meant, but it kept our faith in the Promise alive.

(TERINA): I planned to fly out to Denver ahead of John and the boys with the sole purpose of finding a place to live while he packed up. Gabriella, our new baby girl, was joining me on the trip. I hoped by the time John arrived with the U-Haul truck, he'd drive it straight up to our new home.

The week before my flight departed, my mom called to share another dream she had regarding us. She dreamt I didn't find a place to stay until I was on the curb at the airport in Denver. I figured with all of our friends in Denver, it would be easy to find a place to stay, but that wasn't what happened. Our friends had opened their homes to other guests. Also, I never heard back from an inquiry I placed with Servant Care regarding a hospitality house in Elizabeth, Colorado, where we could stay temporarily as we searched for a home. With four days to go, I still had no place to stay.

The day I left for Denver, everyone asked me, "What are you going to do? Where are you going to stay? Aren't you completely stressed out right now?" I had seen God provide last-minute so many times, so I chose to believe God would provide. I had enough money for a few days' hotel and a rental car, so we were on our way.

When Gabriella and I landed in Denver, I grabbed our bags and scanned the baggage claim for a familiar face. If my mom's dream was prophetic, I would find someone by the time I reached the curb at the airport.

Somewhat disappointed in not finding anyone I knew, I went outside to catch the shuttle bus to the car rental facilities. As I stood on the curb, waiting for the shuttle, my phone rang. I recognized the 303 area code but had no idea who it could possibly be.

"Hello," I said curiously.

She said, "Hi, this is Alice. I own the home in Elizabeth you inquired about a few weeks ago through Servant Care." Typically, Servant Care serves as the liaison between the homeowner and the person requesting lodging. Since she couldn't shake the burden on her heart to know if I had found a place, she called Servant Care to find out what happened to our inquiry. They informed her I was most likely already in Denver based on the date I requested and had no further information. She got my number and immediately called me.

After she introduced herself, she said, "Where are you staying?" I told her I was planning on staying at a hotel." She said, "No, don't do that. Come on out here. I'll whip up some burgers, and we will figure this out!" I told her I looked forward to meeting her and couldn't wait to tell her the full story.

Immediately following, I called my mom to tell her what happened. We both marveled, and Servant Care ended up sharing our story of God's faithful provision in their newsletter.

Alice was one of the sweetest ladies I'd ever met. She exuded hospitality and love. I told her our story and about the dream and the timing of her call. We both rejoiced in God's faithfulness. She told us we were welcome to stay until we found a place. I had no idea how long it would take.

(TERINA): After nearly 3 weeks in Denver, we still were without a place to call home. School had started, but our kids couldn't register until we had an address to identify the district. Solomon and Miki's high school soccer season was in full swing, but they couldn't practice until we enrolled them in school. Yet, not a single rental opened up. We needed a miracle. Our salary, well below the poverty level at that point, kept owners from renting to us. We were out of options.

I rose early one morning and drove to the coffee shop to look for a home online, pleading with God the whole way. Surely God knew we couldn't live with Alice forever! Browsing through the rental section on the computer, I quickly made an appointment to see a house that had been listed 20 minutes before. After the walkthrough, we realized it was perfect for our family; we handed in our application and prayed. As we left, the realtor informed us there were 15 other applicants. My heart sank into despair. John and I both knew that unless God performed a miracle, we were bound to be homeless. We waited all day, but the call never came; we were discouraged beyond belief. I planned on looking up section 8 housing in the morning and questioned, with 7 of us, how that would work.

It was late in the evening when the phone rang. The owner of the home was on the other end of the line. She said, "I haven't been able to get your family off my mind all day. The place is yours if you're still interested!" After hanging up the phone, I cried tears of utter relief and joy. We had a home!

(TERINA): If I could use one word to best symbolize the season looming before us, it would be the word "manna." The word "manna" in Hebrew means, "what is this," or "what is it." We found ourselves asking the same question often: "What is it" we were doing in Denver; "What is it" we had done wrong to be in this position; "What is it" God was teaching us. "What is it" the prophecy really meant? "What is it" we are supposed to do next? The whole season was filled with many questions, but no clear answers.

Even more, manna wasn't only symbolic of our season; it was also what we lived on, like the Israelites, whom Moses commanded, "to collect enough manna to feed them *only* for that day." Anytime the Israelites collected extra to save up for the next day, the manna would spoil and turn to maggots. For us, anytime we attempted to collect anything to carry us over into another day, be it funds or food, our plan would be spoiled. I would later call this term "maggots on tomorrow's manna."

(JOHN): We knew prior to moving in that rent would be a daily walk of faith. We never knew where it would come from, and it was never early! Moving into our house in August, I was relieved to know I wouldn't have to worry about rent until November since we had two months' rent specifically set aside from the previous football season. Yet I hadn't discovered that in this particular season, God only wanted us to collect enough for today, and our extra was about to be spoiled.

(JOHN): I was heading to Oklahoma for my grandma's funeral when I found out our friends were two weeks late on their rent for September. I told him I would pray for God to provide. It was a phrase we heard all too often ourselves, every time we tried to raise financial support for the ministry! Everyone generously offered prayer support, but when it came to giving financial support, such offers weren't so generous.

As I got off the phone, I felt God asking me not only to offer prayer but also to *provide*. I had enough in my bank account, and God wanted us to give it away. Doing so meant we would have nothing for next month's rent, only a few weeks away. We could have reasoned how it was reckless and foolish to do such a thing, but from what we read in scripture, it was this kind of reckless giving He commended (Luke 21). He didn't commend the wealthy who gave out of their abundance but the widow who gave all she had. He was teaching us to give sacrificially, in a way that required absolute trust in His future provision even when we had no idea from where it would come. We ended up handing back tomorrow's manna, as joyfully as we could, to trust He would give us enough for each day.

(TERINA): Rent was provided in October and every month that followed. It was always unpredictable, and it was never early! December is an example of how it happened, month after month.

It was December 31st, and rent was due the next day. My sister was attending a New Year's Eve party her work had thrown, where party-goers gambled with $5000 chips. Unaware of my situation (we don't shout it from the rooftops), my sister casually said to the guy next to her, "You know, even one of those chips would really bless my sister's ministry. You wouldn't even know it was gone!" Somewhat to her surprise, he said "Okay!" My sister called me from the party to ask where he could donate. When we received the donation, it was designated "$3000 ministry, $2000 for you." I wondered if he was an angel, not to say that angels gamble, but how in the world did this happen? It was not only the largest donation we had received but also a donation from a complete stranger. Month after month, God showed up in amazing ways! Our faith grew exponentially as we were not simply reading about His faithfulness, but living it.

(TERINA): My heart sank as I opened the cupboard to find nothing but some beans, rice, and a few other items. I cried out to God, "What is it" You are doing?

During my Bible time, He answered that question by leading me to Luke 9, where He sent out the disciples, instructing them, "Take nothing for your journey, no staff, nor bag, nor bread, nor money; and do not have two tunics." Luke 9:3

Jesus sent them out empty handed so they would be utterly dependent on His faithful provision every single day. This was also how God dealt with Israel in the wilderness, supplying them with just enough manna for the day and allowing any extra to spoil.

At the end of Luke, we see Jesus ask the disciples, "When I sent you out with no moneybag or knapsack or sandals, did you lack anything?" They said, "Nothing." In this season, we had no choice but to learn of His faithful provision, not because we knew a paycheck was coming or we had a savings account to draw from, but simply because He provided our needs on a daily basis. We too could say, "We lacked nothing!"

(TERINA): As always, the prophecy was on our radar, and with each passing week, I'd stand, shovel in hand, digging the grave I planned to bury our Promise in again at the end of every long season. I was becoming a serial grave-digger.

One night, John and I were at the LeTourneau's for a night of prayer when a leader visiting from Bethel Church prophesied over us. They saw a vision of John holding a football in his hand and silver confetti everywhere. And similar to the staff in Moses's hand that brought deliverance to the people, so too, would the football in John's hand. They prophesied over him that he would be one step quicker, and God would give him a father's heart and a young man's courage. God would use us to bring hope, purpose, and restoration to the players and their wives.

It seemed as though every time we were just about to give up, God would send another word, giving us the hope and strength to press on. Though the fulfillment of the prophecy didn't happen this season, we had been given another word to spur us on.

There was a time when we knew nothing about prophecy. But now, given a fresh word from Him specifically regarding our lives, situations, and trials was like giving starving person bread. It sustained our very lives. We were no longer living on bread alone, but "on every word that came forth from the mouth of God." (Matthew 4:4).

I was so incredibly thankful for this amazing gift of His Spirit and was distressed over the fact so many others in the church weren't experiencing His gifts in full measure. Like us, prior to our 1st Prophecy, others too, had never heard a fresh word from God. Churches we attended across the country neither discussed the gift of prophecy or operated in it. The purpose of prophecy is to build up and encourage the body of Christ, and it never failed to do exactly that in our lives. Why weren't we receiving this most valuable and critical gift from Him? I felt like we were eating the crumbs from the Master's table by not partaking of all His Spirit gave us.

(TERINA): God used our time in the wilderness season to teach us to trust Him daily, not the manna itself. Isn't that our tendency? We forget His daily faithfulness and attempt to gather tomorrow's manna today. This isn't to say that saving up is wrong or sinful; it's essentially good biblical stewardship. But we must be careful to avoid our tendency to find "security" in knowing we have enough for tomorrow—finding more comfort in the manna than the One who provides it. This season not only taught us that but also laid a foundation of faith for the unseen trials yet to come.

CHAPTER 24

DO NOT GIVE UP

"Let us not grow weary of doing good, for in due season we will reap, if we do not give up" ~Galatians 6:9

"Then Jacob was left alone, and a man wrestled with him until daybreak. When the man saw that he did not prevail against Jacob, he touched his hip socket, and Jacob's hip was put out of joint as he wrestled with him. Then he said, "Let me go, for the dawn is breaking." But he said, "I will not let you go unless you bless me." ~Genesis 32

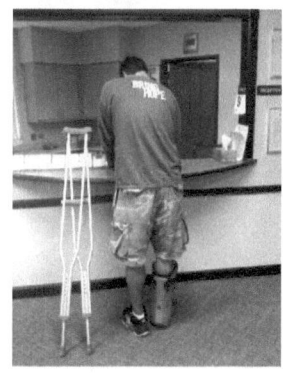

(JOHN): It had been a year since I stepped off the Arena football field for the last time, and the break was exactly what I needed. In the fall of 2012, one of my former coaches from Colorado, who was now the Head Coach of the San Antonio Talons, contacted me about coming to play for his team. I told him I'd think about it, but I was pretty confident at this point that I was done with the Arena Football League.

At this time, Terina and I contemplated moving to Uganda. Since my first trip in 2008, I knew we would be involved in ministry there one day, and we wondered if now was the right time. We prayed and discussed it, but after a few months of talking with the coach, we decided to go to San Antonio instead. While the paycheck would make a significant difference in our financial situation, we felt it was a great opportunity for me to continue to lead the Bible study with the younger guys on the team and invest in them. Football also provided the opportunity to share our ministry work with a larger audience. It seemed to be an open door.

As a couple, Terina and I made the commitment from the beginning of my career to stay together as a family, no matter what. We know a strong family unit is the most important gift we could ever give our kids, so we chose to sacrifice the convenience of not moving the family around to be together instead. There is always a trade-off, but being together as a family is something we have never regretted. Once we made the decision for me to play one more season, I left for training camp, and Terina packed up and prepared to move to San Antonio. I noticed a few days into camp we had a good team; I anticipated the start of the season.

My boys were becoming old enough to really understand football and were excited to watch me play. They asked if they could drive down early with my dad in time to catch the 2nd game of the season. I couldn't wait for them to get here.

(TERINA): Though I usually never missed a game, I stayed back to pack up our entire lives again and was planning to head down in a few days. Meanwhile, John's dad, Jim, planned to send me frequent updates, via text, throughout the game.

Next thing I knew, Jim was calling me from the game. It had become my automatic response to assume something happened, and my heart raced as I picked up the phone. As soon as I answered, I heard, with a tone of utter disbelief, *"You're not going to believe it!"*

"Should I hang up?" I thought to myself. I wasn't ready to receive any more bad news! I sat there in suspended silence, reminding myself of the Bible verse I frequently quoted as a personal reminder, "They will have no fear of bad news, their hearts are steadfast, trusting the Lord." Psalms 112:7

After taking a deep breath, I asked, "What happened?"

(JOHN): The game was in full swing, when, once again, *it* happened. I was in the middle of a pass when I felt a pop in the back of my calf. I knew exactly what it was this time. I immediately dropped down to my knee, knowing I had just torn my other Achilles tendon.

I couldn't fathom it just occurred, *again*; I was shocked. I found my dad and the boys in the stands and signaled for them to come down so I could break the news. I then hobbled back to the locker room to inform the team doctor as well.

(TERINA): After Jim informed me that John just tore his other Achilles and that he was done for the season, I stood there in shock. I stared at our entire lives, stuffed into the boxes I had just packed up to be hauled to our next destination. I hadn't even arrived there yet, and it was already a dead-end road! I didn't know what to say.

After the game, John called me to tell me the news himself. We were both dumbfounded, and for the first time in my life, I was speechless. Trust me, that is significant! Anyone who knows me knows I *always* have something to say. I couldn't muster up a word of encouragement, a scripture, a sorry, anything. We both simply held the receiver to our ear and sat there in utter silence.

When I arrived in San Antonio, John was preparing for his surgery. When our eyes first met, we just looked at each other in disbelief. I still hadn't found words of encouragement to share. The well was dry.

(JOHN): After my second Achilles surgery in just over 24 months, I knew my career was over. This was it! At my age, I would never come back after both Achilles being torn, and everything in me knew the prophecy had to be over as well. I sat there looking at the Keep the Faith plaque we had been given less than two years before and had no idea what to do with it. What was I keeping the faith in? I hadn't lost my faith in God himself, and the plaque wasn't about having faith in the fact there is a God. The plaque was given as a reminder to keep the faith in the Promise He gave us. I just didn't know how to do that at this point. I was lost.

(TERINA): To date, it felt like the hardest season yet, though I think we said that every season! I'm not sure if it was the compilation of everything, but I wondered how long "yet lower still" applied. I felt like a stump. He had cut off the bad fruit, the branches were pruned and placed in a heap to be burned, the trunk was hacked down, and only my tiny little stump remained.

I was reminded of the prophetic word we had received so many years ago where He said, "For every step you tried to take up hill, you were going downhill." *We certainly were.* "Just when you thought you were bottoming out, you hit bottom." *We definitely felt we were at rock bottom.* "But you are on the rebound." *The big question was, would there ever be another rebound?* I needed to hear from God, so I rose early in the morning to read my Bible and pray. This particular morning, God was about to breathe life into the very dry places of our faith again.

It started with a Bible study I felt God highlighting to me. It was a study on Jacob, and with both of John's Achilles tears, I contemplated whether this was indicating something. Often, when you think of the Achilles *heel* in the Bible, you think of Jacob. As I studied his story, I read in Genesis 32:9-11 where Jacob is praying to God, and he reminds God of the promise He had given Jacob, 20 years prior, repeating twice, "*But you have said.*" He was standing firm on the word God had given him years before as he headed back to his homeland and feared his brother. I got to the section where the study examined Jacob's wrestle with God, when it hit me, "John's 1st prophecy!" The first words we ever heard from the Lord coming out of the mouth of the prophet that miraculous day 14 *long* years ago and after John was injured in Cleveland were, "There was a man named Jacob I wrestled until the point that his hip was dislocated." God had tied John's circumstance with Jacob, though even now, I was unsure what it meant, but I knew it was significant. I spent the rest of the morning writing down Jacob's story and how he wrestled with God but prevailed, saying, "I will not let go until you bless me."

He would not let go!

In that instant, I could feel God saying, "*He did not let go!*" *Do not let go, do not give up*! We were supposed to fight, to contend for our blessing, for our Promise. We were to not give up!

I discovered the transition that took place in Jacob, going from one who strived with God to one who clung. His combativeness became dependence, and when Jacob's strength and his ability to overcome on his own failed, he clung on and received the blessing by grace. God had to cripple him to bless him, and it was in his weakness where Jacob learned to cling to God alone. It was exactly what God had been doing in us all these years.

Jacob came to a place where he could do no more but say, "I won't let go until you bless me." Jacob prevailed. He didn't give up! I enthusiastically wrote it down in my journal and couldn't wait to share it with John. God was encouraging us not to give up.

I closed my Bible and journal and turned up the volume on my computer to worship, and as the volume increased, the song "Penuel (Face to

Face)" by Rick Peno had just started. The first words I heard flowing out of the speaker were, "Jacob was alone and wrestled with the angel until the breaking of day, and he named the place Penuel. And he said, I have seen God face to face, and my life was preserved."

I couldn't believe it. For the first time ever, God brought the story of Jacob to my attention, and from it I recalled the first prophecy where Jacob and John were connected, and as soon as I finished my journaling, I turned up my volume to hear these words stream out.

(JOHN): I was confined to the 3rd floor apartment for 3 weeks because my team doctor didn't want me to risk re-injury until my Achilles had a chance to heal more. Though I felt like I was in prison, our family spent a lot of time together. Typical of how God works, He used this time for good, and our family became much closer. All 7 of us were in tight quarters, and we only had each other. The adjustments of the adoptions had been difficult at

times, and at one point, we discovered our oldest two boys weren't even speaking to each other. They would go a week or more without saying a word. Terina and I prayed, "Lord, do whatever it takes to bring them together." God did just that during the time we spent trapped in the apartment. He knit us together as a family, and through being completely isolated, our two older boys realized that friends come and go, places we live come and go, teams come and go, but family is intended to be permanent. After their past, it was easy to understand how they couldn't grasp the concept of permanent family, but we wanted them to feel the stability of that, and God made it happen. Not only did their relationship permanently change after this season of our lives, but they are still great friends to this day.

(JOHN): In regard to football, a part of me wishes I'd never gone back, but in regard to what Athletes for the Nations was becoming, for some reason each Achilles tear expanded the vision. Not only could AFTN partner with athletes of all ages and levels, but also AFTN could partner with schools, ministries, and projects to raise funds for them as well. The ultimate goal wasn't simply to raise funds for us; it was to make athletes significant. I never understood why I had to go through the injuries to develop these ideas, but for whatever reason, that was the case. While developing Athletes for the Nations cost me personally, we could see God's hand constructing it, piece by piece, trial by trial, into all He had planned for it to be.

(JOHN): I was preparing to start rehab on my Achilles tear when my former team doctor in Cleveland, Scott Singer, offered to do it. The thought of living in San Antonio so far from home and the kids being holed up in the apartment for the next 8 months of rehab wasn't ideal for our family. The kids rejoiced when we informed them we were headed back to Beulah Beach.

(JOHN): While this game ended up being the last game of my career, I knew the Promise still stood, and if God really meant the NFL, I would play again one day. Understanding this didn't make the way I ended my career in the AFL easier, but I decided not to let go of the Promise until God fulfilled it. I would not give up!

CHAPTER 25

BELIEVE

"Blessed is she who has BELIEVED that the Lord would fulfill His promises to her" Luke 1:45

"Behold, I am doing a work in your day, you wouldn't even BELIEVE if told" ~Habakkuk 1:5

(TERINA): Prior to leaving San Antonio, I checked on available housing at Beulah Beach. I spoke with my friend Christine, who said, "We are completely full this summer. *Nothing* is available! But, knowing you guys, something will open up!" Sure enough, a place opened up for all but one week of June, though nothing was available for July—*yet*. We knew God was leading us back to Beulah and would provide lodging somehow, so we left for Cleveland. The Waldo Family was on their way again!

How nice it was to be back! We spent 3 weeks catching our breath in a cozy little cottage, surrounded by our friends and the community of

Beulah Beach. John started rehab on his Achilles, and the kids jumped right back into life with all their friends. After the wilderness season we had just been through, He led us beside still waters yet again.

Our housing situation was still up in the air for the 1st week in June and the entire month of July. While there, we found out the camp directors were leaving for vacation the exact day we needed a place and returned the very day our cottage opened up again. It was perfect timing, down to the very days of our arrival and departure. In August, the home we had lived in off and on for a few years became vacant. It was the only stable home our kids knew. Since John's recovery would be long, it was a gift of grace from God. Surely, the Lord does, "lead us beside still waters and restore our soul." (Psalms 23).

(JOHN): Before we left Cleveland to go to Denver in 2012, we told a number of our friends at Beulah Beach about the Promise and our belief it was possibly time for its fulfillment. Now that we were back, I'm sure people wondered what happened. We were still wondering as well! Here I was, a 38-year-old athlete with 2 torn Achilles and a herniated disk. Was He really asking us to believe He would fulfill the prophetic word given to us so long ago?

(TERINA): Wrestling with the Lord regarding our Promise consumed me. What we felt God was saying flew in the face of all reason, yet we wanted to remain faithful to trust Him. Israel didn't inherit their promise because of unbelief. I could relate to their struggle to believe His word of the Promised Land—as time passed, our giants in the land were big. Though I received the Bible study on Jacob, I was again questioning if the prophecy itself still stood. Did we believe John would play football again? Had we lost this Promise and, like Israel, would we perish in the desert due to all the years of our wavering? How would we know?

(TERINA): I was attending a retreat for adoptive moms where I had a table set up for our ministry. The theme of the retreat, Luke 1:45, "Blessed is she who *believes* that what the Lord spoke to her would come to pass," was printed out on a postcard for every attendee. I decided to keep it in my journal as a reminder to continue to *believe* that what God had spoken would come to pass.

This Bible verse was spoken in regard to Mary, who, being a virgin, had an encounter with a heavenly messenger who told her she would become pregnant by the Holy Spirit and give birth to the Son of God. Can you even fathom what it must have been like for this young virgin girl to receive a message like this? There had been a few hundred years of silence between heaven and earth when suddenly God sent the most incredible message ever given to the world to a young girl, from a meager family, living in an insignificant town. (John 1:46) She had no frame of reference, as nothing like this had ever happened before, yet she *believed* God was going to fulfill it. In the same way God asked her to believe in an absolute miracle, God was asking us to *believe* His word, no matter how impossible it seemed. I clung to this Bible verse in hope.

As the years went by without even a glimpse of the Promise coming to fruition, I tried to remain faithful to *believe* God really could do anything, even something as miraculous for which we were keeping the faith. At times, I thought God meant something other than the NFL, but the plaque we were given was in direct response to a prayer asking God specifically about John and the NFL. His response was Keep the Faith. As hard as it was, we were trying!

On the first day of the conference, I was looking at pieces of handcrafted jewelry at the Compelled Designs exhibition table next to me. The incredibly gifted artist made each piece to raise money for adoptive families and ministries around the world. I found a gorgeous ceramic bracelet I wanted to buy that was shaped in the form of a cross with the continent of Africa stamped onto it and a heart stamped over Eastern Africa. It was the perfect bracelet for me. I didn't have my wallet on me, so I planned to come back to purchase it. However, when I came back the next morning, it was gone. The artist explained she sold all the ones she had. I continued checking back all weekend for a different style I liked, but my heart was set on *that* bracelet.

On the last day of the retreat, she told me I could have any piece for only $10. As I eagerly walked over to her table, I spotted the bracelet I originally wanted. I exclaimed, "Oh, my word, it's here! Did you find another one?" She said, "No, where did that come from?" At that point, I didn't really care; I was excited it was there and purchased it. A Bible verse was etched underneath it, but I had no idea what it was. I would look it up when I had a chance.

Later in the day, as my friend and I drove back to our cabin, a song from her playlist was playing on the radio. The few words I heard gripped me as they sung about dreamers who were hanging onto hope by a thread. Since we only had a minute drive or so, I told her, "I want to hear this whole song. Will you play it for me on our drive home tomorrow?" Since certain songs became critical throughout this journey in giving us hope and faith, I looked forward to finding any new song that encouraged us regarding our situation.

The next morning, as we were driving home, I had forgotten about the song. About an hour into the drive, it started playing on her radio.

I asked my friend to start the song over and turn it up so I could hear every word. The song is, "To the Dreamers" by King & Country. While cruising along, I listened to the lyrics carefully, feeling my spirit rise with every word.

It came to the bridge of the song, which repeats the words "I believe, I believe, I believe, I believe, I believe," 5 times. At the exact moment the bridge streamed out of the car speakers and flowed through our car, we drove by a HUGE billboard with a single word written across it in all caps. It simply said BELIEVE.

As I fixed my eyes on the sign and listened to the words, I thought about the theme verse of the weekend, where Mary *believed* God. I thought to myself, "God, are you telling me to *believe*?"

A short time later we stopped to get lunch. While I was standing in line waiting for my order, I noticed the lady in front of me had a tattoo behind her ear. As I inched closer to see what it was, it became clear. I simply saw the word, *BELIEVE.*

It was like the movie *Evan Almighty* where Evan sees Genesis 6:14 everywhere he goes. This time, however, it wasn't a movie; it was really happening. After lunch, we continued on the road trip, and I was reading a word my mom had sent me, and in it was a Bible verse God gave her for me.

It said, "Look around at the nations; look and be amazed! For I am doing something in your own day, something you wouldn't *believe* even if someone told you about it." Habakkuk 1:5

Surely, if God was really going to fulfill the prophecy the way we thought, it was without a doubt unbelievable, but He was still beckoning me to *believe* it anyway. I didn't pay attention to where this verse was located in the Bible; I just sat there and marveled at the events that transpired all day.

Later that night, I was lying in bed with my baby girl curled up in my arms, asleep. My arm was pinned under her head, so I reached around to take off my bracelet when I noticed the verse on the bottom again. I reminded myself to look it up later.

After all the kids were in bed, I communicated to John how God had confirmed the word *Believe* to me over the course of the day. I couldn't recall the exact verse I read from my mom in the car, so I pulled it up. It was then, I *saw* the Bible verse.

Habakkuk 1:5.

"It couldn't possibly be," I thought to myself as I jumped up and ran to the room to get my bracelet from the retreat off my nightstand. I scooped it up and turned it over to see, inscribed on the bottom, Habakkuk 1:5. It was the same verse!

The very same verse my mom randomly sent me was inscribed on the bottom of my bracelet from the retreat, the retreat I got the postcard about Mary believing God, the same weekend I listened as the lyrics "I believe" were repeated 5 times, as we drove by the billboard with the word BELIEVE written across it. It was the same day a lady stood in front of me, not an hour after the billboard incident, with a tattoo behind her ear of the word "BELIEVE."

The Lord was going to do it, in spite of how unbelievable it seemed. Our role was simply to believe.

CHAPTER 26

SUCCESS TO SIGNIFICANCE

Peter began to say to Him, "Look, we have left everything and followed You." Truly I tell you," Jesus replied, "no one who has left home or brothers or sisters or mother or father or children or fields for me and the gospel will fail to receive a hundredfold." Mark 10:29

"I'm going to lay a foundation...You are going to look back and say this is the best thing that ever happened to you... The only thing worse than success is success without me, and I spared you from that" ~1st Prophecy

(TERINA): Known as the "Pearl of Africa" and the "breadbasket of Eastern Africa," Uganda is a picturesque country full of magnificent wildlife, incredible beauty, lush landscapes, fertile farm land, and the location where the headwaters of the powerful Nile River are unearthed. Standing in stark contrast is the unfathomable poverty, both physical and spiritual, that rob individuals, families, and communities of their dignity, worth, health, sustainability, and lives. It was this country, attempting to recover from decades of war, that God would send us next.

(JOHN): At this time, we were in the process of opening another guesthouse/outreach center in Uganda, which was still in the initial building process. God's providence was on full display over the course of the year the guesthouse was being built as He faithfully sent people from the states to assist in setting it up one piece at a time. Our friends, the Vaughn's, with their children, roughed it in the unfinished house for a few months. Arriving when dirt still covered the floors, they laid the concrete and tile, built a kitchen, and put in the bathroom, among other jobs. Prior to their departure, another family arrived and took over the process for a few months, leaving at the end of summer. We didn't know who would go next until a young girl, who wanted to serve overseas, contacted us. She was able to move to Uganda precisely when the current family was scheduled to depart. We wondered whom God would send next, not realizing it would be us.

(TERINA): After John completed rehab, we both felt God leading us to move to Uganda to expand our ministry, but each time we contemplated making a move like this, another door would open up for John in football. This time, he was offered the offensive coordinator position for the L.A. Kiss, an expansion team in the Arena Football League. The decision whether or not he accepted this current offer became a battle of Armageddon-sized proportions between John and me. In all of our moves, it was the first time we were divided. We both felt led to go to Uganda until this coaching opportunity presented itself.

(JOHN): I always felt I would naturally transition out of playing football and into coaching. While I coached at the high school and junior college level, being offered the offensive coordinator job in the Arena League was an incredible opportunity. I wrestled with staying and coaching or heading overseas. The lure of a great career move and a paycheck was challenging to turn down. I reasoned coaching was the right opportunity for our family and for our stability. Deep down, however, I knew the coaching position was what I wanted, not necessarily what God wanted. Though it was an unbelievable opportunity in my eyes, I turned down the offer and followed God's plan. We were on our way to Uganda.

(TERINA): We had no idea when John laid his football career down, like Isaac on the altar of sacrifice, it would be *the* action launching him into his destiny. He wasn't born to play football; he was born to be significant, to make a difference in the lives of others. His talent in football gave him the opportunity to impact lives in a unique way.

After our decision to go, others said, "You can't take your kids out of their school and their community!" "Your husband can't turn down a job. What will you do?" "Shouldn't you wait until your kids graduate?" "You're crazy to bring a one-year-old there!" While it sounded reasonable, I knew obedience trumped all reason. If God says to go, GO! We pulled our kids out of school, removed them from club soccer, turned down John's job, and "dropped our nets to follow Him."

Landing in Uganda was surreal. Everything from the climate, elevation, topography, culture, transportation, food, music, and hospitality were different than Ethiopia. As we walked out the doors of the airport, we were nearly smothered to death by the heat. A mere 48 hours before, we were in the middle of the polar vortex in Ohio, living in sub-zero temperatures outside, and we arrived during Uganda's hottest season of the year, experiencing a 90-degree change in weather instantly. Living in this weather, with no air conditioning, and sleeping under mosquito nets, which trapped in all the heat, would be an adjustment for all. I pondered how my kids would adapt, particularly our one-year old baby girl. It's one thing to bring older kids, but a one-year-old? I did my best to trust God with this one.

When we moved to Ethiopia and now, the same two questions ran over and over in the back of my mind: "What would we go through here?" "Would we all come back?" Living overseas presents many unknowns and additional dangers. While statistically it is more dangerous to drive down the highway in America with my family than live in a 3rd world country, the latter *feels* much more life threatening. I prayed for God's protection, for the ministry work ahead of us, for wisdom and direction, and for our family to return back to this airport alive and well at the end of our time here.

(TERINA): A very special person was waiting for us upon pulling into the gate of our guesthouse. His name was Kakaire, an orphaned boy John and I had sponsored for the last few years, who desperately wanted a family. We were in the process of becoming his legal guardians, and from the beginning, he called us Mom and Dad. Our boys couldn't wait to meet him, immediately welcoming him in as one of our own.

(JOHN): Kakaire was a member of a local soccer team. During our first weekend in Uganda, our boys watched him practice at the local field. When they got back, Miki, one of my older boys, reported that the director of Kakaire's team wanted to meet with me. The next day, after watching Kakaire's game, we met with the pastor. He shared his vision for the team, which matched our vision for Athletes for the Nations exactly.

God had been shaping the vision of AFTN over the prior 4 years. We envisioned developing a sports academy for boys to receive elite level athletic training, but more importantly, to be developed into men of God who used their platform on the sports field to be significant in the world. To find another pastor/coach already doing this through his academy was an unanticipated blessing.

Immediately, I became very involved with the team. We rented property in town that served as the AFTN training center where I trained both Kakaire's team and another high-level club team in the area. I developed their strength, footwork, agility, and conditioning, and then they practiced their soccer-specific skills with their soccer coach. After practice we held a Bible study and ate together. With many of these boys from fatherless homes, it was an incredible opportunity to pour into their lives.

After the first day of holding practice on our new property, Terina and I looked at each other and marveled. The long-awaited ministry of Athletes for the Nations had come to fruition and was transforming the lives of athletes around the world.

(JOHN): As a society, when we think or talk about success, our thoughts and words land on how much money someone makes, what they drive, the house they live in, the status they have. In athletics, it is the same. We measure success by our stats, points, touchdowns, wins, and championships. It is easy to get caught up in the self-focused nature of our societal definition of success, forgetting the purpose behind it.

Though at times I wished I had made it in the NFL in 1999, I see all God has done in and through me. I am so thankful God gave us a detour. Sure, I would have had a "successful" life, but is that what it's all about? Would Terina and I be together, would we have our children, would we be involved in mission work, and would we have 2 adopted sons? Would I have been willing to give up everything for God, or instead been satisfied with giving pieces, leftovers? And ultimately, would I have ever learned of His faithfulness or had the relationship I have with Him now? I don't think so! I thank Him for sparing me from that!

(TERINA): The process of dying to ourselves—our dreams, our plans, and our life, and giving them back to Him for His purposes, His plans, and His people—was painful. But it's what Jesus did. He paid the ultimate price on the cross, giving up everything for others. Aren't we called to Christlikeness? I could no longer give God pieces of my life. Leftovers. He gave His all. So would I.

(TERINA): To see Athletes for the Nations come to fruition was incredible. It embodied John's entire testimony, making every single trial we had walked through worth it. This is what God had been creating all along! Our lives were no longer constructed on a foundation of self that was based on our careers, our name, our pocketbooks, our savings account. Our lives, instead, were newly built on the foundation He was laying, where our gifts and talents were no longer self-serving but to be given away. Every injury, every setback, every trial had led us to understand this. Could we ever fully learn to see every trial and setback as His goodness, not only in the past but also in the future?

Surely we look back and know it was the best thing that ever happened to us! And while we marveled in all God had shown us so far, we had no idea He still had much more to teach us in the pearl of Africa.

CHAPTER 27

WHAT ARE YOU BUSY WITH

"I'm going to use you in many African nations to lift the destitute from the dust" ~Prophecy in Ethiopia

"Is it a time for you yourselves to dwell in your paneled houses, while this house lies in ruins? Now, therefore, thus says the LORD of hosts: Consider your ways...My house that lies in ruins, while each of you BUSIES himself with his own house" Haggai 1:4-6,9

(TERINA): As I sat on my balcony with a cup of hot coffee in my hands, I glanced over at the trash dump (my 2nd floor patio coincidently had a fantastic view of it) and spotted something that never failed to make my heart stop: people *digging* in the trash. I couldn't take my eyes off of the shoeless man, half naked, who leaned over the side of the dump, peering in. I wondered what his story was, where he lived, if he had children,

and even more than that, why the circumstances he was born into would lead him to a place where finding food in the trash was how he nourished his body. Three kids came over and scoured through the rubbish, grabbing and examining treasures they found, then put them up to their mouths...to eat.

At that very moment, my kids were sitting at the dinner table, finishing a warm meal. I tried to reconcile how such a disparity existed between our lives. How can there be so much poverty, lack, and hunger in this country when so much abundance exists in America. While I know "the poor will always be with us" (Matthew 26:11), I knew Jesus didn't state this to excuse us, His hands and feet, from our personal responsibility to act on their behalf. In the *Poverty and Justice Bible*, over *two thousand* verses spell out God's attitude towards poverty and justice and the actions He expects us to take. This is clearly an issue close to God's heart.

It was nearly time to put the kids to bed, which would begin a nighttime routine of hot showers, brushing teeth, and tucking them in to their warm, soft beds. I rejoiced in the fact my nightly routine didn't consist of hiking to obtain sticks and chopping them up to start a fire to heat water for the sponge bath for my children. Bathing consisted of turning the handle and watching clean, hot water pour out. I didn't put my kids to bed on the dirty ground, affording rats the opportunity to nibble on their toes and malaria infested mosquitos easy access to their still bodies as they slept. Instead, I lay them on a mattress off the ground, complete with a blanket, pillow, and mosquito net.

As I observed the scene at the dump, I heard God ask, "*Do you see My House, My people: they are in ruins! Their lives and families are in ruins.*" *(Haggai 1)*

I felt a heaviness engulf me as I felt the burden of His heart impressed on me through more questions: "*What are you doing about it? What is my church doing about it? What are you (as a collective body) busy with?*

In the Old Testament, God's house, and His presence, dwelt in the temple. However, in the New Testament, we became the temple of God (2 Corinthians 6:14-18, Ephesians 2:19-21, 1 Corinthians 3:16-17). His house was no longer buildings consisting of wood, concrete, and stone, but flesh and blood—the people His Spirit dwelt within. As I reflected on his questions to me, I saw these people differently: as His literal dwelling place. And vessels carrying His presence did *not* belong in the trash. "*My house is in ruins. What are you busy with? Really, what are we busy with?*

A fire was developing in my heart, and I could not quench it. I didn't want to. I could no longer tolerate my inconsistent and occasional half-hearted, apathetic response to seeing the destitution of my brothers and sisters.

1 Timothy 6:18 instructs us to "command the rich to use their money to do good, to be rich in good works and generous to those in need, always being ready to share with others."

I knew God was giving us a new assignment: to be His mouthpiece to the American church, challenging them with these same questions, and I knew it started with John and me. We examined ourselves, "Are we busy building our own house, our kingdom on this earth, or His?" When we die, will the things we spent our time and money on impact lives *eternally*? *What are John and I busy with?* It is easy to be busy with our own house, never realizing we have unintentionally placed His house, His people, on the back burner.

(JOHN): This realization led us to more research, both by gathering statistics and looking deeper into God's word. We discovered results that both surprised us and gave us hope. The problem doesn't lie in the lack of resources but in the way they are being distributed, which is something we can change. It's time to consider why American Christians have been entrusted with an incredible amount of wealth.

"I have been generous to you so that you can be generous to others."
2 Corinthians 9:11.

"To whom much is given much is required." Luke 12:48.

(TERINA): This is a principle seen throughout scripture. He entrusted His people with much for a purpose greater than self. When God placed individuals like Esther in the palace, it wasn't merely to enjoy the luxury, comfort, and pleasure the palace provided, but to risk her own life for those outside the gate, though she initially didn't realize it. When Mordecai presented her with the life or death situation of the Jewish people, she replied with a valid reason she was unable to do something, or so she thought. At this point, she was blind to her purpose in the palace. After Mordecai sends her a strong rebuke, even challenging her safety, and opens her eyes by stating, "Who knows if perhaps you were made queen for just such a time as this?" (Esther 4:14 NLT) The realization of her purpose in the palace causes her to respond.

Joseph was elevated to the second highest place in Egypt not simply to enjoy the high position and all it afforded, but to save a nation from starvation, including his own family and the Jewish people.

"God has sent me ahead of you to keep you and your families alive and to preserve many survivors." Genesis 45:7 NLT

And we have Moses who chose "rather to be mistreated with the people of God than to enjoy the fleeting pleasures of sin." Hebrews 11:25 ESV. He willingly chose to leave his position in the palace to save his people. Each individual was purposefully placed in a high position for the sake of others, and so are we. America is the palace, and the American church is rich!

Though American Christians make up only 5 percent of the church worldwide, we control 50 percent of global Christian wealth, bringing in an income of $5.2 trillion a year. American Christians spend over $300 billion a year on things like bottled water, cosmetics, coffee, sporting events, diets, our pets, weddings, boating, golf, eating out, vacation, and remodeling our homes. And if you don't think you're rich, consider this: If your income is $25,000 per year, you are wealthier than approximately 90 percent of the world's population! If you make $32,400 a year, you are in the top 1% in the world in wealth! Does this shock you?

To show the global impact these resources could make, consider the following: It would take just a little over 1 percent of the income of  American Christians to lift the poorest one billion people out of extreme poverty. Twenty-five billion dollars would relieve global hunger, starvation, and deaths from preventable diseases in five years. Fifteen billion dollars would solve the world's water and sanitation issues. When reading these statistics, one must ask, "How is the church stewarding its resources?" Are we investing them into His house, or are we like the rich man, who Jesus warned of in the parable in Luke 12:13-21, investing them in our own?

"The ground of a certain rich man yielded an abundant harvest. He thought to himself, 'What shall I do? I have no place to store my crops.' "Then he said, 'This is what I'll do. I will tear down my barns and build bigger ones, and there I will store my surplus grain. And I'll say to myself, "You have plenty of grain laid up for many years. Take life easy; eat, drink and be merry."' "But God said to him, 'You fool! This very night your life will be demanded from you. Then who will get what you have prepared for yourself?'

"This is how it will be with whoever stores up things for themselves but is not rich toward God."

I spoke with a professional athlete regarding a conversation he had with a teammate about attempting to raise funds for his charity. Frustrated at the lack of giving, this player, who made nearly $20 million that season, stated, "I'm beginning to think I should just pay for it myself." You think?! What else is it for if not so that you can be generous to others? Not to say we shouldn't be wise or save, nor does this mean we should never enjoy any pleasure, remodel our home, go on vacation, own a pet, or spend money on ourselves. Of course not! Once again, it's a heart issue of storing up for ourselves while *not* being generous towards Him. Billy Graham stated, "Give me 5 minutes with a man's pocketbook and financial records, and I will tell you where His heart is." We know, "Where your treasure is, there your heart will be also." (Matthew 6:21 ESV). I pray our pocketbook reflects our desire to build His house above all else.

His house, His people lie in ruins all over the world. They are in brothels, slums, trash dumps, mud huts, hospitals, on the streets, in our foster care system, and in orphanages.

What are you doing about it?

As God laid our foundation, we discovered turning our success to significance wasn't the final step. We can live lives of significance without His kingdom being our first priority. Many of us unknowingly pursue positions, platforms, success, material abundance, and our own pleasure more than we do His. It is time to ask ourselves, "What am I busy with, and how will I respond?"

CHAPTER 28

STEP INTO THE PROMISE LAND

"For it is no empty word for you, but your very life, and by this word you shall live long in the land that you are going over the Jordan to possess."
Deuteronomy 32:47

"There was a man named Jacob that I wrestled to the point that his hip was dislocated..." ~1st prophecy

(TERINA): I was visiting our ministry partner, Tsige, in Ethiopia. We were both fasting and praying about what God had next for us personally and as a ministry. As we walked the dusty back streets of Ethiopia, something incredible occurred.

The night before, I flipped through a book I had previously read called *The Dream Giver* by Bruce Wilkerson. The book is about Ordinary, a nobody who leaves the land of Familiar to pursue the purpose of his life, his Big Dream. Once the Dream Giver convinces him to escape his comfort zone, Ordinary begins a difficult journey to find out what His big dream is, but must travel to the Promised land to find it, overcoming Border Bullies (which in real life would include concerned family and skeptical friends) attempting to stop him from leaving the land of Familiar, the wasteland (wilderness), and the giants in the land before finally arriving at the place he would discover his dream.

After reading about Ordinary's journey to his promised land, I prayed a prayer I have prayed for years, *"Lord, when is it time for us to enter into the Promised Land? When is it finally time?"*

It surprised me when, a mere 18 hours later, someone suddenly appeared to my right, in my peripheral vision, singing. He was a young Ethiopian man, and as he passed by us he sang two sentences, in perfect English, and then continued on his way.

"Step into the promised land... Walk into the promised land!"

I looked up, shocked. "Did you just hear what he sang?!" I exclaimed.

In Uganda, it's common to hear English amongst the locals, but in Ethiopia, English is not as common, particularly when singing. For some guy, on a back road in Ethiopia, to walk by and sing *those* words in perfect English the day after reading that book and praying that specific prayer was profound to me.

(JOHN): During the first month in Africa, I developed excruciating pain in my back and down my leg, making it difficult to walk or sit down. As much as I tried to push through the pain, I knew something was wrong and decided I needed to see a doctor. There was a physiotherapist from Germany who had set up a practice in Uganda. Upon being examined, he noticed that my hip was out of place.

(TERINA): When John called me and told me, it hit me. God wrestled with Jacob *until* the point when his hip was dislocated. Did this symbolize that John's wrestle with God was over? I shared the story about the words the Ethiopian man sang as he strolled by us on the back roads of Ethiopia and thought, "*Could it be?*" Were we finally at the border of our Promise? Was it time to step into the Promised land?

(JOHN): We still had 10 months to go in Uganda before returning to the states. Our ministry was experiencing a lot of transitions, both with starting new projects and transitioning out of old ones. We had arrived in Uganda right before the presidential election and had been monitoring the situation closely. Anytime there is an election in a country like Uganda, there are always threats of uprisings. While all of our friends had evacuation plans in place due to instability, rioting, (no, American riots do not come close) and talks of a potential coup, they advised us that it was moderately safe to come for now, but to have exit plans just in case. Needless to say, we were on edge.

(TERINA): One evening John and I heard loud popping noises and immediately jumped up, screaming, "Get in the bathroom and lock the doors!" while rounding up our children and bolting to our room. We were certain it was a coup. After seeing bright flashing lights outside, we noticed the fireworks. We laughed when we discovered that was all it was. Who in the world had fireworks *here*? We were that on edge!

(JOHN): Our remaining time in Uganda tested our faith, perseverance, and commitment as we endured car accidents, lawyers running off with thousands of dollars and extorting us, mob justice, and numerous terrorist attack threats. We were stolen from several times, and our whole family battled homesickness and physical sickness throughout. We pushed through numerous power outages, the water being shut off for weeks, no air conditioning, sleeping under mosquito nets, and a few encounters with deadly snakes on our property, including cobras and black and green mambas. We couldn't even relax when our kids ran in the yard. One night, our son Drew stepped on a baby cobra with his bare foot, and miraculously, it didn't bite him. With the hospitals closed that late at night, I can't imagine what would've happened had it struck him. If God can shut the mouth of a lion, he can shut the mouth of a snake, which is exactly what He did.

As adults, we can push through these challenges, but watching your kids go through it is difficult. They all grew so much in their character, perseverance, and strength, but it certainly tried us. By the end of our stay, we were definitely ready to head home.

(TERINA): After living in a third-world country with your children, nothing makes you want to cry tears of joy more than hearing the words, "Welcome to the United States of America." I couldn't believe I was hearing those words! Landing on American soil felt like we had entered the Promised Land.

As I walked through the airport, I wanted to sing "God Bless the USA" at the top of my lungs while marching through the airport waving a flag. I could hardly contain my joy. I felt compelled to hug strangers and couldn't wait to breathe the fresh air of freedom, to drive on roads where there were lanes and stop lights and my life didn't flash before my eyes at least half of the time! I couldn't wait to buy all the foods our family had craved and to feel a sense of safety again.

America is far from perfect. Corruption and sin exist no matter where you go, but the principles of freedom, individual rights, and justice for which our country stands are unique. I completely took it for granted. In places we have lived, there is no such thing as 911. If a robber breaks in, all you can do is hide or hope he doesn't attack you. Often the police are working with the robbers, so reporting the case doesn't necessarily bring justice, either. There isn't a judicial system where you necessarily have the right to a trial. While they do have trials, they also have the authority to throw you into jail for things like a broken windshield or a missing rearview mirror, without a trial at all.

A guest at our house stopped a street kid from being lit on fire after getting caught stealing because mob justice is how crimes are punished. John attempted to stop an incident of mob justice outside our gate, but with a mob surrounding him, he was unable to stop them from beating the man and performing mob justice. People often confiscate land, even from widows or orphans. No justice system is set up to ensure they get it back. One staff member moved with her family from Kenya, and when her father died, their "pastor" and the local LC (the police) confiscated their family home and worked together with officials to create new documents naming themselves as the owners—and got away with it. Her family lost everything. The power company can bring two separate power bills, one a ridiculously high, made up amount you "owe," and the other a much cheaper option if you're willing to give them a bribe. We refused to pay bribes.

Traveling was always stressful, not only because it was dangerous but also because if you do crash, you are typically looted, not assisted. Our friends were in a car accident. As her husband lay on the ground and she hung sideways, dangling from her seatbelt, over 20 people looted their car, taking money out of their wallets, opening the glove compartment and taking anything of value, never once offering to help. The amount of corruption at every level creates a survival mentality where everyone is out for themselves, and often, those in positions of power join in, doing nothing to enforce laws and protect the people.

The injustice of it all made me want to hug and thank every law enforcement officer I ran into when we returned home. Seeing the effects of a culture running rampant with so much crime and corruption made me incredibly thankful for law enforcement here in the U.S. and the men and women that help to preserve justice, security, and freedom for its citizens by their work.

The first thing our kids wanted was In-N-Out, and we headed there straight from the airport to get burgers. They were so happy. If stepping into our prophetic "promised land" was any better than this, I couldn't fathom the joy we would feel! Though we knew it would take a miracle, God had said "miracles would happen." We were ready.

CHAPTER 29

MIRACLES WILL HAPPEN

"I am the LORD, the God of all mankind. Is anything too hard for me?
~Jeremiah 32:26, NIV

Miracles will happen. ~Prophecy in Ethiopia

(TERINA) Many times, we want to see God perform the miraculous in our lives, but we forget the place we may find ourselves in before a miracle can occur. Often when we read of miracles in the Bible, someone was deathly ill first, or they were surrounded by foreign armies determined to destroy them, or they were placed in a situation they could not escape on their own. The cost of a miracle can be high, and it will push our faith to the limit. For us it was both.

On a snowy morning, we were driving down a small highway on our way to church, when a truck, attempting to brake before the stop sign, hit ice and instead slid right out in front of our car. It happened so quickly, there was nothing we could do to avoid T-boning his truck. I screamed, "John!" and braced myself for impact. I knew we weren't simply going to hit this car; we were going to slam into it, and we did, totaling our vehicle. The sound of impact terrified me, and as I waited for the chaos to ease and our car to stop, all I could think of was my children (all 5 of them) in the back and what was happening to them. As we came to a stop, my heart was beating rapidly, and I braced myself for what I would see when I turned around. Were my babies okay? *OH GOD!*"

I turned around and looked at my little girl. She seemed okay, but my attention immediately turned to Drew, then 10, who was screaming at the top of his lungs. I looked at him and saw his head was bleeding. It didn't appear to be a major wound, but he was in a lot of pain, and there was blood. I tried to stay calm. I reminded myself that even small head wounds could produce a ridiculous amount of blood, so I wasn't overly concerned with the amount until he continued crying and shouting, "My head, my head hurts, my head!" in a piercing sound that penetrated down to the very core of my being. My boy! John jumped out of the car and struggled to open the door where Gabriella was, so he ran around to my side of the vehicle while I continued scanning each child to make sure they were okay.

While John was assisting Drew, a lady ran up to our car. This was *God's first little miracle* because she was a critical care nurse (of course), who was on her way to church when she pulled up to the scene of the accident. She immediately attended to Drew while we waited for the ambulance to arrive. She noted that all his vitals were good, which calmed me as I assumed everything was okay. I knew that Drew had a concussion because he was completely unaware of what was going on, repeatedly asking the same questions over and over, and had no recollection of the past few days. But after being married to a football player and having been around multiple concussions, I was familiar with it so I reasoned he would be fine. The nurse mentioned the gash in Drew's head being a concern, but we felt good knowing she was there to help. Once the paramedics arrived, they put him in a neck brace, laid him on a spinal board, and put him in the ambulance (all procedure). By the time he was loaded into the ambulance, his symptoms had progressively gotten worse, and he went from crying in pain and saying, "My head hurts," to becoming more incoherent, not being able to answer questions as clearly and becoming more unresponsive. My concern was beginning to grow.

I asked if I could quickly tell my husband to grab his phone at home as he didn't have it on him, but they responded, "No! We need to go now!" That alarmed me. I couldn't take 10 seconds to make sure he had a phone? "Is everything fine?" I asked. They stated because he was not responding coherently and due to some of his symptoms, their concern for internal bleeding on his brain was growing. I went from calm, or possibly in shock, to a full-on panic in an instant.

Once we arrived at the hospital, Drew continued to worsen to complete incoherency. Strapped into the spinal board, he was throwing up all over himself. It was on his face, in his hair, and in his ears, so they tipped the board sideways so the vomit wouldn't choke him. He lay there lethargically, with his neck wrapped in a brace, his eyes glazed over, and not responding to my voice; my heart ached so badly for him. It was the worst sight I have ever seen as a mother. He didn't even attempt to wipe off his face. At this moment, I prayed the words, "God, *have mercy* on my boy."

I went to lightly brush my hand across his tummy in a circular motion to comfort him, and as I did so he shrieked in pain. When the nurse saw his response, she asked if he had been wearing a lap belt. I had to think for a moment but realized he had, and the next thing I knew, other nurses and doctors were alerted and came rushing in. Due to the lap belt being on his stomach and his stomach being in so much pain, they were concerned for internal bleeding and did an ultrasound and took X-rays. While we waited for the results, I needed to let John know where to go, and the nurse assured me that unless there was internal bleeding he would remain at this hospital. John still hadn't arrived, and when the results came back, they determined he needed to be airlifted to the Children's Trauma Center immediately.

I sent out urgent prayer requests and loaded up in the helicopter to fly to Cleveland with my boy in the back. Just as we were on the helipad, I saw John pull up, but I didn't have time to talk to him. I shot him a quick text, telling him where we were headed. Once we arrived, my heart broke to see Drew being taken out of the helicopter. I couldn't believe I was watching *my* child being unloaded from *this* helicopter, the one that symbolized someone in a critical state every time I'd ever seen it in the air. I did everything I could not to completely lose it emotionally. When they wheeled him in the trauma room, there were at least 8 doctors waiting for him. They immediately set him on the table, cut off all his clothes, and began working on him.

At this point, I felt like I was having an out-of-body experience. *"Is this really happening? I can't believe this is happening right now!"* At the same time, I felt such a supernatural peace. Truly, there is *"the peace of GOD that surpasses all understanding."* (Philippians 4:7)

I knew that God was sovereign and was ultimately in control of everything. I reminded myself of how many people were praying. Little did I know at this time just how many people actually were. My sister, who was a finalist on American Idol, is a recording artist, and has her own hunting show, posted a prayer request on her fan page that was viewed by 35,000 people and had over 500 comments. We were on prayer chains all over the country and even the world, as some of our African friends were praying as well. I knew that prayer was powerful as *"the prayer of the righteous avails much."*

I had personally seen miracles of healing before and had prayed for people who received a complete healing. Reading about a God who heals is one thing, but personally witnessing Him doing it is another! I reminded myself of His power, over and over, while I watched 8 doctors working on my son.

Quickly after arriving at the Children's Hospital, I began to notice a significant change in Drew. He became alert, his eyes were no longer glazed over, and he was beginning to answer questions coherently. He was speaking more clearly, and his memory appeared to be coming back.

When they pressed on his stomach, the place where I laid my hand to gently rub it before, he had *no pain* whatsoever! It was that moment I knew God was doing something.

John had to drive 45 minutes by car to get there, and by the time he arrived, Drew was alert, answering questions more clearly, and was much more responsive. He still had no recollection of the accident or why he was at the hospital, and he was still repeating the same questions, but he had improved drastically from briefly before. I began thanking God while continuing to send out prayer requests and updates.

As we sat in the room, we watched as Drew transformed before our eyes. He started to remember my answers instead of asking the same questions repeatedly. He no longer complained about his head hurting, and I knew things were different when he suddenly started joking with us. It was remarkable.

I told John, "The doctors have no idea what a turnaround he has made since the previous hospital." Only a few hours after being airlifted to the trauma center, he had improved so dramatically he was released to go home!

The whole way home, John and I sat there amazed. Did all of that just happen? We praised God for hearing our prayer. We have seen God heal other people, but it was a gift to receive His mercy and healing on our own son.

When I lay in bed that night, I couldn't help but feel so blessed. I don't know why God showed mercy on Drew, which is what I prayed for as he hung sideways on that board throwing up, but I am so thankful and humbled He did. I can only attest it to the prayers of all the people.

In a single day, I went from my son being life-flighted to a trauma center in Cleveland to him lying sweetly next to me in bed with his head bandaged and still suffering a concussion, but okay.

I woke up early the next morning to read my Bible. As I randomly opened my Bible, the first thing my eyes landed on was the title, *"A boy was healed,"* in Matthew 17. It instantly caught my attention. I began reading the story, and read where the father in the story fell before Jesus and pleaded, *"Have mercy on my son."* (Matthew 17:15). Those were the exact words I muttered as Drew threw up all over himself the day before. At the end of the story, it says, *"The boy was healed that very hour."* I began to cry! I just knew God was telling me He had, in fact, healed Drew that very hour as I prayed for His mercy. It was a miracle!

As I reflected on the events of the previous day, I heard God state, "This is the beginning of miracles." I was more excited than I had ever been. To step into the Promised Land, we would surely need a miracle. But after this, our faith was fully persuaded God had the power to do what He promised. We were ready!

CHAPTER 30

WRITE THE VISION

"My words . . . will come true at their proper time." Luke 1:20

Write the vision; make it plain on tablets, so he may run who reads it. For still the vision awaits its appointed time; it hastens to the end—it will not lie. If it seems slow, wait for it; it will surely come; it will not delay. Habakkuk 2:2

(TERINA) I got a text from my mother-in-law saying, "I think you're supposed to be writing a book called *Keep The Faith*. It caught me off guard, as I thought, "Does she know anything about the book?"

Four years prior I was lying on my bed, studying the Keep the Faith plaque so miraculously given to us that day, and God impressed it upon my heart that the story surrounding the plaque would become a book one day.

I had been recording our story down in my journal, but I kept to myself what was in my heart. It felt somewhat arrogant, even embarrassing to say, "I think there will be a book about our story one day," as though our story is anything special, which is what surprised me about receiving that message from my mother-in-law. I wrote her back and asked, "Did I mention anything about a book to you?" "No," she responded. "Since you live such a life of faith, I feel like you should write about it." I knew it was time to begin formally writing the book. I had no idea how to complete a book with an unfinished story, so I prayed for God to show me the next step as I began the process.

After arriving back in the states, we waited 4 months for a home to open up for our family and spent the meantime driving up and down the West Coast between John's parents and mine. While passing through the town of our good friends Rick and Wendi Cross whom we hadn't visited for a few years, I sent a text asking if they would be around at the time we were driving through. She informed me she would be at a writers' conference. Curious, I asked her about the conference and told her I was actually in the beginning process of writing a book. She encouraged me to attend, but when I looked into it, I realized it was impossible, as the retreat was almost $1,500. We were missionaries and didn't have $500 to our name, let alone that amount. I immediately let it go. A few days later, she asked if I looked into it. When I told her my discovery about the cost, she mentioned the idea of applying for a scholarship. I applied, and a few days before the retreat was set to begin, I got a call stating I could get 40% off. I thanked them for their incredible generosity and told them I would discuss it with my husband. After getting off the phone, I cried. I was so tired of being unable to afford anything though we worked so hard for years. After years of pouring ourselves out and receiving little pay, it is beyond discouraging. I prayed, "God, if you want me to go, you have to make a way." The following day, the camp called to offer me a payment plan for the next 8 months. That I could do! I registered, and 2 days later I left for my first writers' conference.

At the conference, we were supposed to present a proposal or manuscript to editors, agents, and publishers. Because I did not have any of the above, I was embarrassed to present the story behind the book to anyone. How do you seriously share a book regarding a Promise that hasn't happened yet?

I felt like Joseph in the Bible, given the dreams from God but still chained in prison and writing the story from that place. (Psalms 105:12). Unless you know how the end of the story goes and how God redeemed Joseph and fulfilled the dreams He gave him long ago, the story *is horrible!* What makes the story of Joseph incredible is God fulfilling the prophetic dreams he had years before. If the story ended when he was in prison, I question if it would've ever found its place in the Bible! I questioned why I was there at all.

I found a publisher whose bent was more toward the prophetic, so I shared the story with her to ask her what to do. I figured she would *maybe* be the one person here who wouldn't think I was irrational. When I began sharing how we were prophesied over, she asked, "Who was it?" When I told her, she responded, "Oh, I know him!"

After hearing the story, she looked at me and stated, "Wow! I have a feeling you have to finish the book before the prophecy comes to pass. First, you shared the prophetic word with the Bible study. The next time you shared the prophetic word with the team, coaches, and staff. This time, you have to share it with the world!" After my heart momentarily stopped beating, I replied, "I was afraid of that!" The next day, a pastor was praying over me and said, "The Lord is impregnating you with this book, and you have nine months to deliver it."

It was exactly what I needed to get moving!

Being new to the process of writing a book, I wasn't sure what my timeline looked like. How long would I need to edit it? Would I self-publish it, or did God have another plan? Would I publish it before we knew the final chapter, or would the final chapter happen right as I wrapped up the book? I had more questions than answers.

I began writing diligently, praying every minute of the way that God would show me what to do next. All I knew is I had 9 months to deliver this book, and I had to be faithful. I had a timeframe for self-publishing, but thought if some rare modern-day miracle were to occur and a publisher published it prior to its fulfillment, I would need a timeline for that as well.

My good friend connected me with a friend of hers from seminary who did some editing for a publishing company. With much embarrassed hesitation, I shared the story behind the book and how it is based on an utterly impossible prophecy that hasn't been fulfilled yet. I expected him to hang up on me or at least laugh out loud; instead he mentioned a publishing company he was working with.

He connected us via email, and for a second time, I awkwardly shared the story of the book I was writing. The consultant at the publisher responded, "I've heard a lot of crazy stories, but this one gives me goosebumps." By the end of the conversation, she gave me a 4-week deadline, which was a direct answer to prayer. I had prayed specifically for a date because I knew the book would never be finished otherwise. Then the real writing began.

Writing this book has been THE HARDEST thing I've ever done! I've cried through almost every chapter as I recalled the painful events of the past 20 years, and with each page, I experienced the doubt still residing. Believing God's Promise, in spite of the impossibility, has been difficult beyond words.

I was on the phone with my mom the night before the manuscript for this book was due, asking for prayer. I told her that I don't know how I'm going to finish this book. It's as though I'm reading someone's story, and, throughout the entire book, I'm thinking, "Man, these people are idiots! Why don't they give up? How foolish can they be?" Then I realize it's our story: My husband and I are the ones still holding onto the Promise in spite of how ridiculous it is. I told my mom, "I need God to give me a confirmation in regard to the book and the fact that I am *really* supposed to be writing it for some reason. Any remaining faith I had before I journeyed back through the past 20 years while writing the book is all but gone. My faith feels lower than it has ever been. If I'm going to complete this book by the deadline tomorrow, I *need* God to send me a confirmation tonight to give me the strength and faith to finish it. Otherwise, I can't wrap up this story of keeping the faith when I feel as though I have none left." My mom told me she would pray for God to give me a confirmation *that very night* to confirm to me He was, in fact, asking me to finish the book.

Not five minutes later, I got an email from a lady who had no idea I was writing a book. This is what it said,

"As I prayed for you recently, the Lord spoke to my heart this scripture:

And the LORD answered me: 'Write the vision; make it plain on tablets, so he may run who reads it. For still the vision awaits its appointed time; it hastens to the end—it will not lie. If it seems slow, wait for it; it will surely come; it will not delay.' Habakkuk 2:2

She continued, "There may come a season when you are weary, discouraged, and even doubtful; keeping His vision in the forefront of your hearts and minds will cause you to remember God's faithfulness, His what, why, and how!"

I was literally speechless.

For us, we still don't know the final chapter; what we do know is that God has said it would be both surprising and amazing. However, we feel like we're writing from the prison place, before the redemption, before the fulfillment. Reliving all the disappointments, failures, delays, setbacks, injuries, stresses and struggles along the way makes the fight to keep the faith harder than ever. It feels like we're foolish to believe the Promise being fulfilled still lies ahead of us.

But we press on. We find the strength to rise yet again and step up to the challenge at hand. Our strength is weak—we are weary! Our faith is wavering, struggling to keep its pulse to stay alive. But in the midst of it all, we are reminded once again, He is faithful. I feel His Spirit move over our valley of very dry bones and breathe life into them again.

The prophecy, the very dry bones, long dead, lying in the desert place, is coming alive again. His Spirit is moving, His breath giving new life again. The army is rising, and this time, we will rise in victory! We will Keep the Faith!

CONCLUSION

DON'T GIVE UP

(TERINA) As I finished this book, I felt God give me this word for you, our readers. Many of you are in the desert place. You feel broken, hurt, lost, angry, and some of you are even in despair. God *is* saying to you: Don't *ever* give up. Don't *ever* give in. I *am* with you. I will *not* fail you. Keep the faith!"

When I began to realize God was leading us not only to write but also to release this book before the final fulfillment, I felt a sense of sheer terror. "*Surely, God, this can't be what you are asking me to do! What if it doesn't happen? What will everyone think?*"

I had been in this place before. When we shared the prophetic word God gave us, ahead of time, both in San Jose and then with the Colorado Crush, we didn't know how it would turn out, and while we try to remind ourselves it's not about us or our reputation, it is still terrifying. I am surprised to find myself in that place once again. I have no idea what God is going to do or how this will unfold, and I can't believe I am sharing it with the entire world ahead of time, but I realized this isn't simply about the fulfillment of our Promise—it's about the fulfillment of yours.

The fulfillment of our Promise will serve as a sign, an indication that God is getting ready to move in your life as well.

As I was writing this, I had a vision of a valley of dead bones, exactly like those in Ezekiel 37. As I saw the valley of very dry bones, the Lord said, "Prophecy to the bones that they would come to life."

These bones represent you. They represent your broken dreams, your broken relationships, your broken marriages; your broken lives. Maybe some of you feel disillusioned and are struggling with purpose, sin, addiction, depression, hopelessness, identity, and defeat. You feel worn down, beaten, and barely breathing. You feel you have lost your way, and it has caused you to doubt God, His goodness, His faithfulness, His power, and, for some, His very existence.

Some of you were given a dream, a promise, or even a prophetic word. You were convinced it was not simply an idea you had; you believed it was God-inspired. But over the years, as the setbacks, disappointments, and failures piled up, you began to doubt it, eventually casting it aside. You threw in the towel. You must have had it wrong, you assumed. You let it die, and with it, a piece of you died as well.

If this is you, *know this*: God is calling John and me, through this book, to prophecy to your dead bones that they may live again.

"Then He (the Lord) said to me, 'Prophecy over these bones and say to them, O dry bones, hear the word of the Lord. Thus says the Lord God to these bones: Behold, I will cause breath to enter you, and you shall live, and I will lay sinews upon you, and will cause flesh to come upon you, and cover you with skin, and put breath in you, and you shall live, and you shall know that I am the LORD." (Ezekiel 37: 4-6 ESV)

We believe this book represents the prophecy to the *bones* and will serve as a catalyst to stir up the dry bones in the lives of many, signaling that it is time for you to shake off the doubt, unbelief, and despair that has caused you to lie down in the desert and let your hopes and dreams die. It is time to rise again. The Lord is getting ready to breathe new life into your broken places, dead places, like He did in Ezekiel 37.

As Ezekiel prophecies to the bones, they begin to come alive and join together, but notice, though the bones came together, "There was no breath" (vs. 8).

They weren't alive just yet. The Lord then commands Ezekiel to "prophecy to the breath and say, 'Thus says the Lord God: Come from the four winds, O breath, and breathe on these slain, that they may live.' So I prophesied to the breath as He commanded me, and the breath came into them, and they lived and stood on their feet, an exceedingly great army."

I believe God showed me that the fulfillment of our Promise will be the indication that God is getting ready to breathe on you once again, and when He does, you will rise, many of you, an exceedingly great army. Hallelujah!

While some of you will read this book and question, doubt, mock, or even flat-out think we have lost our minds, this is written for those who would dare to believe in the miraculous. For those who would have the faith to believe God is faithful to keep His word to His children and can do anything. Even more, He is getting ready to fulfill not only His word to us but also to *you* as well.

God is getting ready to move. God is saying, *"Now is the time!"* I hear excitement in His voice, anticipation in revealing all He is about to do. Let the dead bones rise! Let the dead places live! Let the dead dreams rise again, for such a time as this!

He will breathe new life on His bride, yet one more time, and when He does, watch the army arise! You are an end-time army, and His plan for you is great.

Don't seek the glory, seek to make Him known. This is going to be the greatest harvest of souls the world has ever seen!

WHAT ARE YOU BUSY WITH

1. (http://www.investopedia.com/articles/personal-finance/050615/are-you-top-one-percent-world.asp)
2. https://www.charismamag.com/site-archives/572-newsletters/the-buzz/3928-the-wealthiest-christians-in-h
3. Global Issues, "Poverty Facts and Stats," www.globalissues.org/article/26/poverty-facts-and-stats.
4. Global Issues, "Poverty Facts and Stats," www.globalissues.org/article/26/poverty-facts-and-stats.
5. Church Leaders, "Generous Church: Top Ten Characteristics," by Brian Dodd, http://www.churchleaders.com/pastors/pastor-how-to/151049-brian-dodd-generous-church-ten-top-characteristics.html.

WE WOULD LIKE TO THANK

God for your steadfast love and faithfulness towards us. May this book bring you glory.

Our parents and siblings for being such amazing family. Your constant love & support is truly a gift from God and our love for each of you is immeasurable.

Our beautiful children Zach, Drew, Miki, Solomon, Gabriella, and Kakaire for blessing our lives beyond measure. This is your story as well and we are so proud of you for being so strong and full of faith through every stage. We love you so much and feel blessed to be called your Dad and Mom!

Our family & friends who stood beside us along the way. Thank you for your grace, love, and encouragement.

Our ministry supporters for your generosity and prayers. We would've never made it without your support.

Our ministry partners Joey & Destiny LeTourneau for blazing a trail & demonstrating a life fully surrendered to Him. You have taught us so much about living a life of radical faith. This book exists in part because of you.

Africa for changing our lives in ways we could've never imagined. We could never repay what you've given us.

Those of you who made this book possible: To Donna, who graciously spent months reading this book from cover to cover and editing every page, to those who made a meal, watched our kids, etc. Words can't express our thanks! We would've never completed this project without you.

Our friends Niki and Mark at Imperium Publishers for your endless grace and patience in seeing this from start to finish. We are blessed to be a part of your team.

www.ingramcontent.com/pod-product-compliance
Lightning Source LLC
Chambersburg PA
CBHW020405080526
44584CB00014B/1179